ISLAND LIVING

God's Plan To Move You
From Isolation to Restoration

SHEILA HARPER & ROBIN GILLIAM

TABLE OF CONTENTS

ECCLESIASTES 4:10

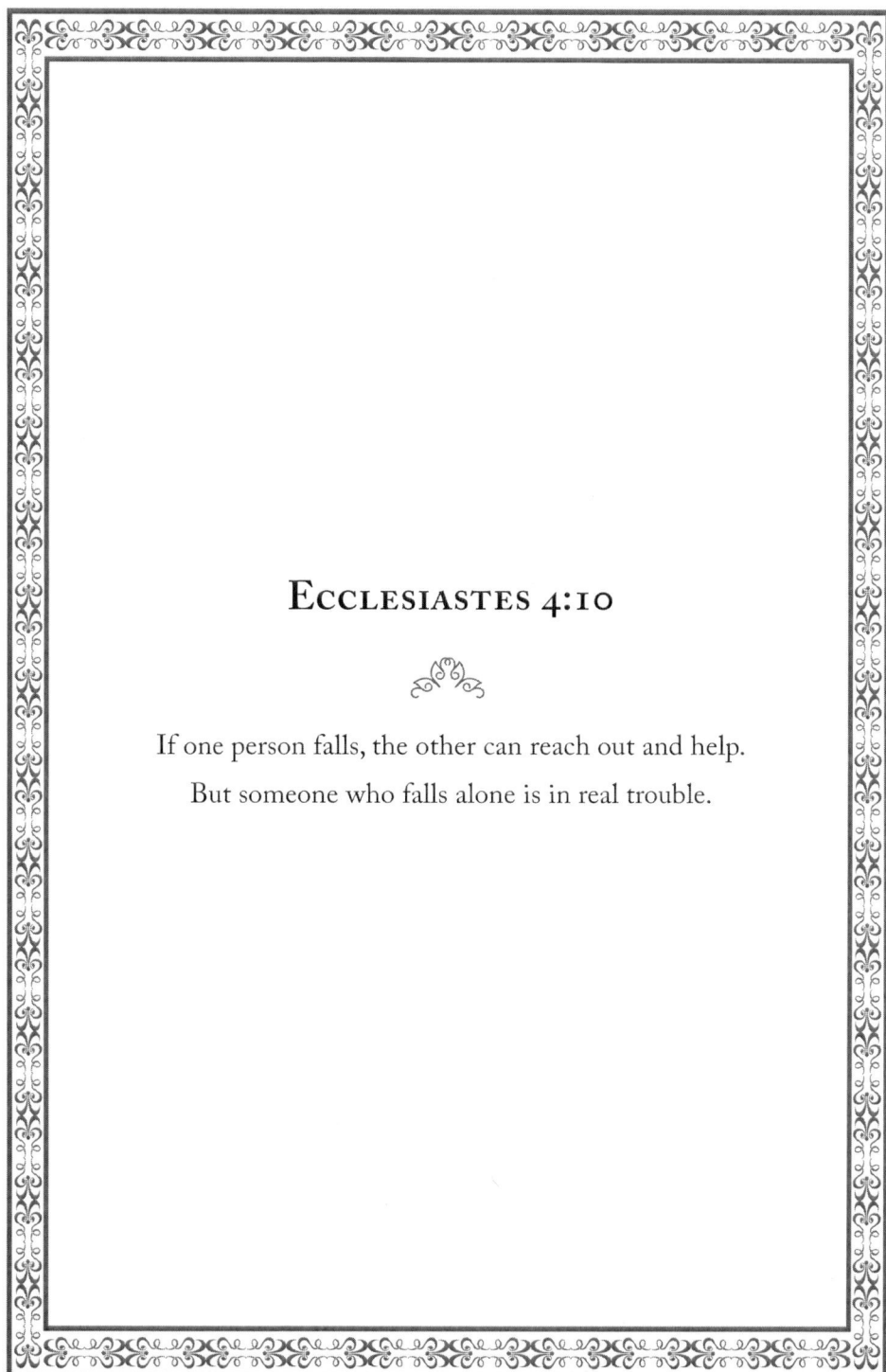

If one person falls, the other can reach out and help.

But someone who falls alone is in real trouble.

A Word from Robin

The day started off pretty good: a long list of things to do like the laundry, cleaning the house, and paying the bills. It was pretty much like every other day. Isn't it funny how a day can start off normal, and BOOM, just like that everything changes?

Jerry walked through the front door and I knew something was wrong. Something big was about to happen. My husband said I needed to sit down, that we needed to talk.

Every woman I know dreads those words. Our minds start spinning, and we wonder about dozens of things. What happened since this morning? Are the kids okay? Are we okay? Do you have a terminal disease or something?

We had lived in Atlanta for eight years, and it was my home. I lived there as a child, and my heart's desire was to stay forever. This day, my dream of staying would change. My husband unfolded the story of how the senior pastor sat him down and told him the church had to let us go due to the economy. They could no longer afford to keep us. My heart sank and I honestly felt like my world was being shaken to the core.

Being a pastor and denominational leader's daughter, I grew up moving every four years. I never really settled anywhere before it was time to move again. You can imagine what this news did to me. I had made many friends and the church was my family. The Bible studies I taught were growing every week. Was this a sick joke? Had God played a cruel trick on me? I sat in my living room and wept. I was so angry and upset. God, why now? We have nowhere to go and no place to consider. My children will have to be uprooted and pulled away from their friends.

As the weeks went by, we went on many interviews, and God eventually led us to a church in Tennessee. Before we went to this church, He made sure to prepare us for what was ahead. As long as I live I will never forget what He told us, "I have prepared a place for you to go, but the journey ahead is going to be very painful. It's going to be the toughest assignment I've ever given you."

What did that mean? Where would we go that would be so hard? Why would God do this to us or allow it knowing we were first-time pastors? Let me tell you this ladies, God wasn't kidding. Our first assignment as lead pastors has been brutal at times.

I am convinced. All my experiences from then until now have led me to partner with Sheila to write this book. We will talk about all the hurts, challenges, and yes, despair we have felt, but we will also talk about the victories and strength God has given us to overcome our struggles. I have spent years looking for books, blogs, and Bible studies to help me understand the hurt, rejection, and identity challenges I have faced as a pastor's wife. The Lord would not let me rest until I wrote this book.

My prayer is that *Island Living* will touch and hopefully encourage you to press in, hold on, and if you have isolated yourself, to rejoin us here on the mainland. We believe you will find truths and validation on these pages as we bare our souls and hopefully help you along the way. God is always working behind the scenes, and He has a plan for each one of us. We're going to make it together. I can't wait to hear from you.

A WORD FROM SHEILA

We were supposed to be celebrating a big day for my husband. He was getting his pastoral credentials and was finally seeing the culmination of many months of intense study. He completed his education while also being self-employed and traveling quite often with his job. He had worked so hard for this day, and I was so happy to be standing by his side at our annual gathering of statewide pastors and their wives. Except there was just this one thing…

This gathering of pastors was taking place in the town where I grew up, in the nicest hotel in the city, which also happened to be the place where I was raped. I thought I could do it. I told myself I'm a new woman. I believed I had convinced myself that I was not that old person who used to be wild, and date men I hardly knew. Little did I know the plans that were being laid ahead of time for my mind and my belief system.

I had visited this hotel bar many times, but always in an altered state. I realized, this time, I was walking back into the hotel sober…for the first time. We knew a few of the people already so we were able to have conversations with old friends. I held it together pretty well until the first service that night. The enemy infiltrated my mind telling me to look around at all of the pastors' wives. They had it together. They had been walking beside their husbands for years doing ministry, without all of this baggage. He started feeding my mind with thoughts like, "You're just a fake…You'll never fit in…What were you thinking coming here acting like you belong?…They'll find out about you…I'll bet none of these other nice ladies have ever committed the acts you have… Look at you, you're really nothing but a fake." The more I tried to fight the thoughts the more rapidly they came.

I made it through the first night and the next day. But then it came time for the "Pastors' Wives Luncheon." My husband had already signed me up and paid for it. Oh, how I feared it. How could I talk to these ladies? What could I possibly have in common with them? What if they EVER found out what happened to me in that hotel?

I told my husband goodbye, and he left to go have lunch with a friend. I made the dreaded walk to the luncheon trying to choke back tears and look happy. When I entered the room a girl at the door handed me a gift. I walked about ten feet further, and the tears started spilling out uncontrollably. I made a U-turn and got out of there as quickly as I could. I burst through the doors to the outside and walked the two miles downtown to where my husband was having lunch, crying, praying, crying, praying, and trying to get in control of my emotions.

I knew I was about to ruin this great time for my husband, and I really didn't want to do that. I was fighting with everything I knew, but nothing seemed to be working. I felt stupid, out of place, and dirty.

When I made it to the restaurant and plopped down in the booth by my husband I instantly felt safe and was back to myself. I made a joke about the boring ladies' luncheon and how he and his friend were much more fun. I wanted barbecue ribs anyway! They laughed it off and didn't question me.

That night was the credentialing service, and I knew I HAD to go, be happy, and celebrate my husband's achievements. I put on my best church smile, wore a killer outfit, and told myself I was going to make it; I could do this! During worship, I completely fell apart. I was broken before God. I told Him I didn't know what was happening. I had never had this kind of vicious attack on my mind. How was I ever going to not be a fake as a pastor's wife?

Suddenly I had a vision. God has given me dreams, visions, and foretold things to me. He speaks to ALL who are listening for His supernatural voice. This night was one of those times. I saw myself in a cone of light. It started small over my head, literally like an upside-down ice cream cone. It was a brilliant light, and I was wearing all white. He spoke these words to me, "This is how I see you. You are holy and righteous before Me."

Tears are falling even now as I remember the complete, enrapturing love I felt from Him at that moment. I knew I really WAS going to make it. I really COULD go be a pastor's wife even with all my baggage and failures from my past. I had a sense of complete peace about the future knowing as long as I'm good with Jesus then everything else is secondary.

Yes, I made many mistakes, and the enemy tried and failed to stop us by making me believe I could never go forward with my husband in ministry because of those mistakes.

Fast forward to today, and we are several years into a church plant. I have had to go back and draw strength from that occasion many times. It is because of that mental struggle, and the many subsequent struggles I have faced as a pastor's wife, that I have realized these stories of victory need to be told.

Robin and I have heard so many similar stories from fellow pastors' wives. We have been told about unbelievable attacks on their minds, their belief systems, and their kids. Ministries, marriages, and futures are being put to the test. We believe that pastors' wives can be the most vulnerable people in the church.

The enemy knows if he can get to you, then he can derail your husband and the ministry you accomplish together.

I write this book with my friend Robin because we have come to realize if we are living these struggles, others must be too. Our friendship provided validation of our own personal hurts and struggles, and where we had gotten to as pastors' wives. We provided for each other a place we could go and be safe, vent without gossiping, and be put back on the right path. Through this book you will be validated in your struggle, given helpful tips on how to overcome, laugh with us about some of the things that have happened to us, cry with us over our very real disappointments, but then close the last page with a renewed strength, a new vigor, a stoked passion, and a realization of victory and who you truly are in Christ.

It is our prayer that these struggles have not been in vain, but rather to point the way to the only place we can all turn for help, Jesus Christ. He is our hope, our peace, our foundation, and our strong tower. He is mighty to save, honoring to His servants, and full of peace and joy.

We can do this ladies...***together!***

ISLAND LIVING EXPLAINED

ECCLESIASTES 4:9

Two people are better off than one, for they can help each other succeed.

Ministry is a wonderful and exciting adventure. You may have always seen ministry as an opportunity to stir a hunger in people. Your heart may be to see others fall incredibly in love with God and go hard after Him. Things don't always turn out the way we think and people don't always respond like we do. Some reject you and others could care less about the time you put into them and their struggles. You see church attendance and God become optional for many and before you know it, you feel like a failure and the hurt begins to build.

There are a few red flags we're going to give you to recognize island living in your own life. Just like the flags, you see waving on the beach and the meaning behind each color, there are visible warning signs that show us we're heading toward an island. Some of the warning signs include a loss of hope, believing things will not get better, and things that before were insignificant now become major issues challenging your peace of mind. You avoid any deep conversations because you don't want others to see your weaknesses. You day-dream about starting a new life, and it seems a dark cloud hovers over everything you do. If we had to give you a definition, island living is closing yourself in, while shutting others out. It is true what the Bible tells us about hope… when deferred, it makes our heart sick (Proverbs 13:12).

In ministry, it is so easy to isolate ourselves. We have valid reasons and wonderful excuses as to how island living occurs. You may even remember the moment in which you got in your raft and floated away. You may realize you have isolated yourself, but you don't know how to make your way back to land. The very real possibility exists that you may not want to because you know you will have to open your mind and heart again making yourself vulnerable to hurt and criticism.

Our goal is to get you off the island and back in the land of the living, not just surviving, but THRIVING! We can't allow each other to get on an island. If we're not careful it's easy to get pushed into this inaccessible place believing no one understands. Only another pastor's wife can really comprehend what you go through. Sometimes we are so wounded we just want to go bury ourselves and hide. But you were not created to walk alone. God's intentions are not to see you deserted on an island. God has a plan to rescue you!

Here are some questions to consider…How did you get on the island in the first place? What triggered your mind to think you are better off alone? If we separate ourselves then the enemy finds an easy target.

FROM ROBIN:

Jerry was watching National Geographic one day, and they were showing water buffalo in a herd. Not far away was a pride of lions. There were only six or seven lions, but hundreds of buffalo. One of the buffalo got away from the herd, and a lion immediately went after it. At the same time, an alligator jumped out of the water and grabbed a leg of the buffalo. The lion grabbed its head and a tug of war ensued for the buffalo. When the herd saw what was going on, they came back united and fought off the attack. Even broken and bleeding they rescued the buffalo, circled around him, and protected him while the lion and alligator ran away.

What an excellent example of what happens when we work inside (and outside) a united community, such as a church family. We are harming ourselves and making the most detrimental mistake of our ministry when we separate ourselves. We feel as if we are protecting ourselves when actually we are doing just the opposite.

Some things that trigger this protective mode of isolation are betrayal, rejection, and criticism. Many times, these actions come from the people you least expect. What we have found in our ministries is that often times the people you pour the most into are the first to dish out this betrayal, rejection, and criticism. The enemy uses these thoughts and feelings against you and makes you suspicious of everyone.

When you allow these ungodly thoughts to stay in your mind you soon are sailing away to that island of seclusion where the enemy will torment. It's easy to go into this "solitary confinement" mode when betrayals have happened multiple times. There are people you trust in ministry; people you give positions of leadership to; people you believe are going to do something great for God, who turn out to be nothing but another name on a long list of disappointments. There is nothing the enemy wants more than for you to start thinking everyone is like that. He wants you to be suspicious of people. He wants you to withhold your best self from the people around you.

Pulling back from those we've been called to lead is detrimental not only to us but the people placed in our lives. God has positioned certain people in our lives for a reason. Sometimes it's to grow us, but other times it's for us to plant seeds inside others and help them grow. While you can't be friends with everyone, you can steward your time with people well regardless of how they treat you in return.

We have written this book to call you out of isolation and into restoration. You are not the powerhouse God called you to be as a pastor's wife if you are living on some island by yourself, doing life in disunity instead of community. You were born for community. You were created for unity. The enemy knows that and wants to keep you from who God has called you to be. We're here to get you up and going again if you feel like you've been knocked down. You're stronger than this, and you are an unstoppable tool in the hands of a powerful, almighty, and sovereign God! There are many people in your tomorrows who need you and will appreciate who you are.

Take these next few days, weeks, or however long it takes you to read this book, and just focus on yourself. Yes, it's going to be okay to just focus on yourself. Get alone with God. Read this book, memorize the scriptures, and allow God to help you walk off this island. Leave loneliness, fear, anger, frustration, unforgiveness, bitterness, and all that is pent up inside of you. Let's walk it out together and drop it in the sand like a bad habit! We did it, and you can too.

The following chapters are battles we have faced as lead pastors' wives. You may relate to some and think we have been living in your house, or you may be surprised that anyone has ever felt the way we have.

There are times we have failed miserably, and times we have been victorious. We have been honest about all of it. We hope throughout these next pages you will find yourself in our stories and something we say will get you off this island of loneliness.

Part One:
Leading Causes of Island Living

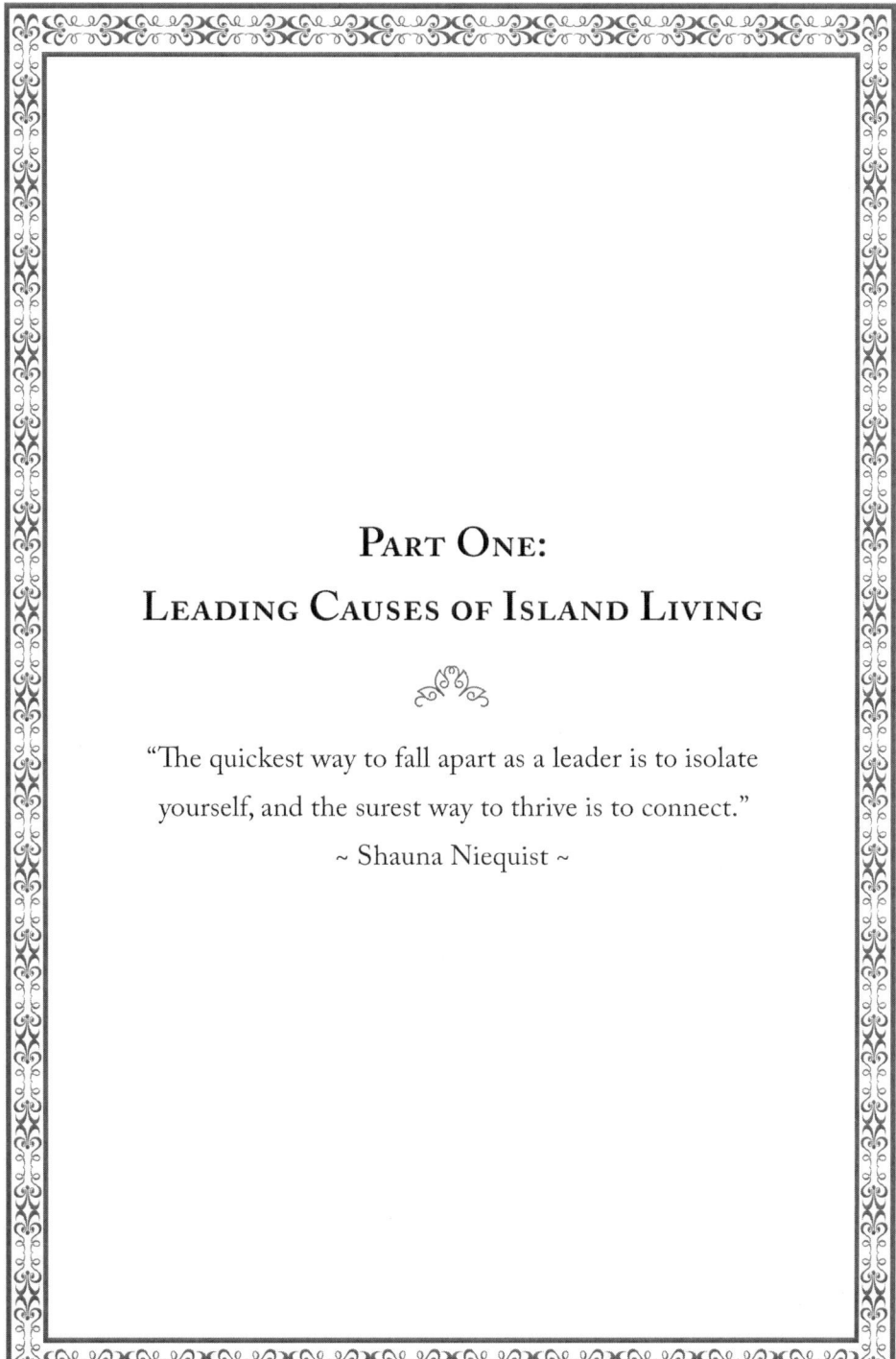

"The quickest way to fall apart as a leader is to isolate yourself, and the surest way to thrive is to connect."

~ Shauna Niequist ~

You think you're all alone. You feel like there must be something wrong with you. "How did I end up on this island, and am I the only one who struggles with these challenges?"

In the book of 1 Kings, you'll see quite a contrast between the Elijah in chapter 18 and the Elijah found later in chapter 19. The differences are startling. At first, Elijah is bold and courageous, victoriously facing all kinds of odds with the chapter concluding, *"The hand of the Lord was on Elijah, and he girded up his loins and outran Ahab to Jezreel."* Elijah was strong and ready; pumped about what he had been called to do.

God gave Elijah supernatural strength to do the extraordinary. But in chapter 19 we find quite a different Elijah. He is depressed, scared, tired, and wanting to die... kind of like he was living on an island by himself, don't you think? As we read these chapters we see the cause of this change in Elijah. King Ahab tells the notorious Jezebel what Elijah has done. He tells her Elijah had all her false prophets killed. She reacts exactly as the king knew she would and threatened Elijah's life. He ends up running for his life all the way to Beersheba where he crawls under a broom bush in deep depression and asks God to let him die. He started looking at the natural instead of relying on the SUPERnatural strength God had given him. He let his circumstances defeat him.

We've all been there feeling defeated and full of despair when everything you lived for exploded right in front of your face. We have no way of knowing what Elijah expected because we aren't told, but something shattered his focus and faith. Just like Elijah, we can hear God's Word and even experience the work of God in our lives and still become scared, depressed, lonely, and full of despair. Elijah was told to go stand on the mountain and God would pass by. When he followed God's instructions a hurricane wind ripped through, and God wasn't found in the wind. After the wind, an earthquake came, and God wasn't found in the earthquake. After the earthquake, a fire came, and God wasn't found in the fire. Finally, after the fire, there was a gentle and quiet whisper, and in the whisper, he heard God's precious voice.

Like Elijah, we will go through seasons that challenge us, and we will go through seasons that make us question everything. But, it's in those seasons His small still voice will bring us back to the knowledge of who He is and what He will do to help us accomplish His will for our lives. We must trust Him even when we don't understand what is going on around us. God has a purpose for every season, and we can rest in His promise to use what we learn, all for His glory. We can't let devastation lead to disobedience.

"As members of the Body of Christ, it is impossible for any part of the Body to function optimally, in isolation. Just as all of the parts of the physical body need one another, the same is true in the Body of Christ."

Excerpt from *"It's Not Punishment It's Preparation"*
by Augusta Reed

CHAPTER ONE
FEELING LONELY

Don't be afraid for I am with you. Don't be discouraged,
for I am your God. I will strengthen you and help you.
I will hold you up with my victorious right hand.

ISAIAH 41:10

The scripture on the previous page is one of our absolute favorites in the whole Bible. We picked this verse because it is so telling of God's love. He never leaves us. He is always with us. And He is holding us in His victorious right hand! Remember this verse throughout chapter one. Better yet, write it on your mirror in a lovely shade of red, and memorize it. Then you will have it in your arsenal when the enemy tries to take you on a sailing trip to the island.

READ-THE-ROOM-MODE

Have you ever been in a room full of people who are actually talking to you but you still feel lonely? Is that because you are the only pastor's wife in the room? Is it because you are worried about the whole picture? Often times there is so much on our minds, we cannot enjoy the people around us.

There are very few times as a pastor's wife you can just walk into a room and enjoy the room. No one is thinking like you do, feels like you do, has had to deal with the heartaches like you do, or carry the weight of others' secrets like you do. We call this state of mind a "read the room" mode. We walk in and read the room by thinking about what is going on with everyone else, instead of just being able to enjoy the people in the room.

Someone in that room may make a comment about "having to make a major decision," and all of a sudden, you're pondering whether or not that decision is to go find another church.

You notice Mr. Hathaway is there by himself, and your mind instantly wonders if his wife really did follow through on her threat to leave him.

You see Sharon on the other side of the room, and you make a note to steer clear because of her constant backhanded complaining about your husband.

You also notice that Kathy who just wrote you that horrible email two days ago is laughing it up with another church member and butterflies hit your stomach. Those butterflies come because you know you have to make nice with her for everyone else's sake without revealing how manipulative and downright mean she is behind the scenes.

Do any of these scenarios sound familiar? These thoughts and feelings make us feel isolated. They are legitimate thoughts and valid feelings, but we cannot let them control us. Those external circumstances keep our minds occupied and keep us from putting our best selves out for others. When we allow the thoughts, and worries of others to infiltrate our minds this deeply, we are never totally present in the moment.

We are the gatekeepers of our minds. We get to choose which thoughts stay in or get kicked out. We have to consistently put 2 Corinthians 10:5 into practice and take our thoughts captive. We do not obey our thoughts or give those negative ones any brain space.

You Are Not God

People are coming to your church because it's a safe place, a place of refuge and healing. As a pastor's wife, you are coming to church and being the facilitator of those things. We know God is the One putting forth the healing and restoration, but oftentimes people look at you as the answer to their problem. When you are not, then they think something is wrong with you or the church. You have to remember there is only one God, and you are not Him.

Often times people tend to think if you, as the pastor's wife, don't pay attention to their need, then that is a problem on your part. Or if your husband didn't do his job to their expectation then they are not getting what they need from the church. You should be going to church for a refuge and safe place too, but as a pastor's wife that all changes.

From Robin:

One Wednesday night we were showing a video series at church, and this particular night the video was talking about what pastors go through. What the pastor on this video was saying was like he had been living at our house! I could relate to everything he spoke of, and it was breaking my heart. I had never heard anyone speak out loud the things this man was speaking. I saw so much of his struggles in my husband and in my heart.

Before I knew it the tears were flowing, and I couldn't get them to stop. He pulled out all the hurts and frustrations I had suppressed. As hard as I tried I couldn't get the tears to stop, even when the lights came back on. I knew everyone there that night saw me sobbing, but yet not one person came up to me to console me. No one checked on me. No one asked if I was okay. Nothing.

I felt lonelier that night than I have ever felt in a room full of people. I went home and cried myself to sleep thinking there was nowhere I could turn to deal with my struggles.

Be The Cheerleader

Pastors' wives also need restoration and healing, but who can we share our inner thoughts with? Many times, we need healing because of the people who are in our church who have mistreated us. We cannot be completely open about our hurts and struggles.

We feel as though we can never be who we truly are because it's not acceptable. People want us to come into the room and be their cheerleader, without thinking about the hard hits we might be getting. These things make us feel lonely because the congregation doesn't have a clue what we struggle with on a daily basis.

Our church family looks to us for stability, consistency, and mentorship. They want us to be their rock; that person they can count on. Honestly, when this position we are in is put into perspective, it is quite an honor. If we are elusive, or an emotional wreck, what kind of example is that? This doesn't mean we never show our true selves, but it does mean we can rise above the attacks that come our way.

Often times one of the greatest combatants for loneliness is being that cheerleader for someone else. This action takes us outside ourselves and helps us get life into perspective.

On Purpose Action

We still feel lonely at times; I think that's just life and humanity. We can't write this book and make you think we have this thing whipped. We also don't want you to continue to feel this way on a regular basis, or you will never reach your full potential. Getting past the loneliness takes "on purpose" action from all of us.

The enemy wants us to believe this loneliness stems from something we're doing wrong. This is not just a pastoral affliction. Everyone feels lonely occasionally. When Robin and I became friends and then started opening up about our struggles and listening to other pastors' wives, it validated us knowing everyone struggles with loneliness in ministry at times.

WAYS WE HAVE FOUND TO COMBAT LONELINESS

We get out of the house and get busy doing something that takes our minds off ourselves.

We call our closest, trusted friend or family member- sometimes a girl just needs another girlfriend.

We blast praise music or listen to our favorite podcasts. At times to get out of a funk, it's good to hear another perspective.

When the enemy is trying to torment, spin that around on him by turning the negative thoughts and feelings into something positive. Take action you know he doesn't like. For example, we may text a church member who hasn't been at church for a while or set a coffee date with a woman from church who needs a friend.

Make a list of all the things you are grateful for.

The main and most magnificent way to fight loneliness is to pray and praise believing God has you. He has this situation you are in, and He is fighting for you.

OTHER COMBATANTS
FOR LONELINESS

Be sure to take care of the practical. Make sure you're getting good sleep, taking a Sabbath (we'll talk more about this later), eating healthy, and checking on your hormones. We could write a whole book on hormones alone, but that's another subject. We have to do all we can to combat any health issues causing a change in our mood or mindset, but then we can also call on the Ultimate Healer to hold us and guide us through this rocky terrain.

The truth is, our fight is in the spiritual realm concerning negative situations that happen with church members. These same members are being fought, too, with things that we may have done wrong or perceived to be wrong. From the members' perspective, the enemy tries to make them feel like they have not been reached out to, they've been hurt by church decisions, or we're not sympathetic to their plight. As validated as we feel, the church member feels just as validated. It's the enemy's plot to divide and conquer us.

The moment something bothers us, if we deal with it with that other person, then so much would get worked out immediately and not allowed to grow. Matthew 18 is an excellent principle to be learned and acted upon when a conflict arises between people.

The real enemy is the devil. He is out to destroy relationships. Our church members are not the enemy. We've been hurt by people, but there are very real explanations for that. Sometimes that explanation is that they're a jerk. But when you realize that, just chalk that up to a "now you know" moment and move on.

From Sheila:

I have been very open with my church family about my past abortion in 1985. They have been very understanding and supportive of the abortion recovery ministry I founded. Not long after we started the church, I signed up to take a ministry team to do sidewalk church to inner city kids. Several other people from my church signed up to do the same. We have a rule in our church though, that if you have ever been arrested for a sexual crime, then you cannot work with children. One of the ladies in our church signed up, and through her background check, we saw she had been arrested several times for sexual crimes.

My husband had the hard task of telling her she could not work on the team that would be working with children, but that we would welcome her in another ministry. She seemed to understand and even admitted she knew the results would probably stop her. I guess she went home and thought about it because her wrath showed up on Facebook. Her post went something like this… "My church turned me away for (and she stated her crime) but they will let someone who has killed their baby work in this ministry…SMH". There were several other remarks, but that is all I saw.

My heart was ripped open, my head exploded, and tears were instantly pouring. I was crushed.

Of course, I kept going back to check on the post and several people had liked it and she had even gotten a few responses about how stupid the church was and how we just didn't understand.

But what really stuck out to me is the fact that not one person from my church defended me. I kept looking and hoping someone would remark and take up for me, but all I heard were crickets. I was horribly embarrassed. I didn't want to take the ministry team anymore, and I was convinced I was an embarrassment to my church. I was completely alone and never wanted to face anybody again.

It was a horribly lonely time for me, and I finally counseled myself off the island. After weeks of mental turmoil about this one Facebook post, I realized not everyone knew she was talking about me. Just because I knew it didn't mean everyone else did. I knew that when you are doing anything significant for God you are going to be attacked and tested.

Going through this incident helped me grow a thicker skin and keep my head up. I can live in shame about my past and get knocked down when people say things, or I can do what God has called me to do. I'm going to choose God every time even if I get punched in the gut occasionally.

Devourer-Back Up Off Me

We named this book *Island Living* because of this very thing. We get hurt, we back away, we feel lonely, and we seclude ourselves, putting us in the perfect position for the devourer to divide and conquer. We cannot let each other stay in that vulnerable spot.

Here is a quote from the book, *When Words Hurt* by Warren Bullock that we feel goes perfectly with what we are saying here…

"But we can withdraw emotionally, using our withdrawal as a shield. It keeps people at a distance from us and may indeed protect us from more criticism. But it also repels those closest to us, those who love us themost. So, through self-protection, we may gain a sense of security but lose the openness to people who have so much to contribute to our lives. Such isolation is counterproductive."

As the leader in your church, people will model your behavior. What kind of example is this for others? When we give in to loneliness we are giving in to the warfare around us. We are losing the battle and allowing circumstances to trump the call on our lives. We have to model behavior that is victorious, not of a martyr or victim. The only way to model this is to genuinely believe in the victory! This, in turn, backs down the enemy and helps him realize you are not some weakling he can mess around with anymore. Living out the knowledge that God is holding us in His victorious right-hand shows the church and the watching world that, as a Christian, we can live joyful, productive lives that change the world around us.

Find A Friend

Pray for and seek out that friend who you can trust; preferably another pastor's wife who completely understands what you're going through. If you do not have anyone, then it's okay to look at a fellow church member and say, "Hey I'm going to partner with you and pray with you, but the truth is I'm having a rough week." You don't always have to give details, but if they know you struggle too, and you don't have it all together at times, then you become more real. Many people will find it a privilege to know how to pray for their pastor's wife.

ANSWER & APPLY

1. Am I being transparent and allowing others to help me?

2. Am I searching for resources dealing with my struggles?

3. Am I open to, and working on developing new relationships?

TAKEAWAY

We are all learning and maturing together during this season. God can be our best friend and He knows us better than we know ourselves. He knew you and yes, He still called you. He knew what He was getting into!

"Believers must always be mindful of the hidden adversary. Although they must effectively deal with people, when encountered with negative situations; they cannot waste time or beat the air by fighting people, rather than the enemy of their souls- the devil."

Excerpt from *It's Not Punishment It's Preparation* by Augusta Reed

Chapter Two

Fear

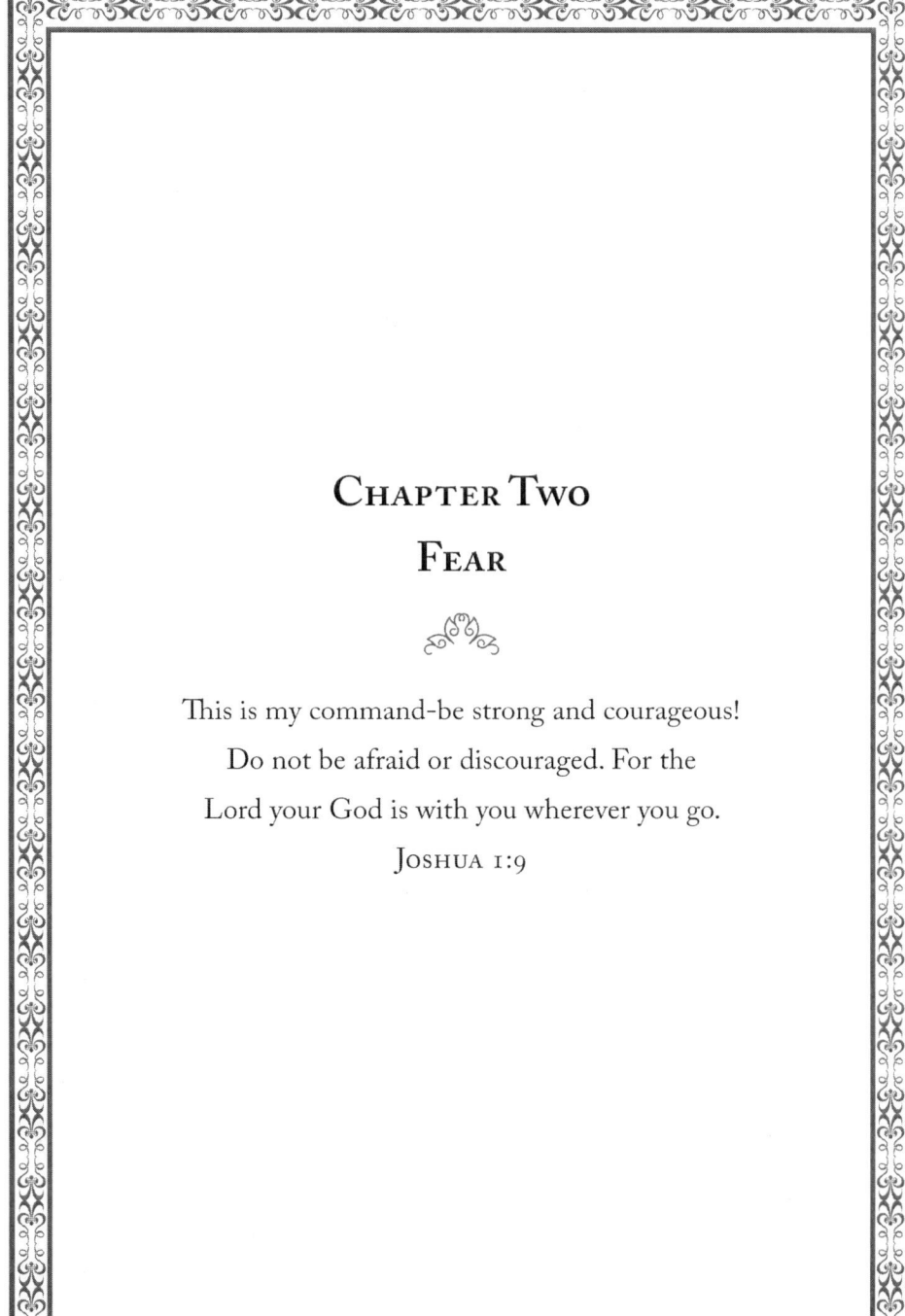

This is my command-be strong and courageous!
Do not be afraid or discouraged. For the
Lord your God is with you wherever you go.

Joshua 1:9

While you're writing out your verse to memorize this week, :) let's talk about fear…Did you know that F.E.A.R. can stand for *False Evidence Appearing Real*? Sometimes we believe it really stands for *Forget Everything and Run*!

What Is Your Fear?

The *Huffington Post* wrote an article that said one of the biggest fears as a society is public speaking and identity theft. WHAAT? We read it on the Internet so it must true, right? Sometimes we put degrees on fear. We may be brave in one area and think others are ridiculous for fearing the very thing we're brave in. Just because a fear doesn't make sense to me or you, that doesn't mean it's unfounded.

You may have opened up to someone and allowed them to see your fears, and they acted like, "What's the big deal?" Their reaction may have made you feel stupid and unwilling to open up to anyone else, so you keep stuffing down the fear, letting it live on the island with you. We're asking you to pull out your fear, look at it, and realize whatever your fear, it's legit and needs to be dealt with through the peace of God that can cover everything.

We tend to look down on other people's fears when their fears do not make sense to us. We may watch an episode of "Hoarders," see the fear on these people's faces when things start getting thrown away, and we just don't understand. Why would they fear such a thing? But then that same episode may show the person who was hoarding, and years later they are happy and living in a clean home. What they feared actually became the greatest thing that ever happened to them.

What are some of your fears as a pastor's wife? We can list ours, and we wonder if you can relate to the fears we've had.

- Fear of people leaving the church

- Fear of not measuring up to an elusive standard

- Fear of making friends in the church and then being hurt by them

- Fear of being compared to the pastor/pastor's wife before

- Fear of an affair

- Fear of damage done to our children by the church

- Fear of not having enough finances

- Fear of not having the right answers

- Fear of lack of attendance

- Fear of failure

- Fear of husband's health digressing

- Fear the church will cut salary

- Fear of lack of provision for retirement

- Fear of being gossiped about

- Fear of being lied to or about

- Fear of being misunderstood

- Fear of declining health

- Fear of being stuck in one place

- Fear of my life being wasted

- Fear that nothing will ever change

Are you catching a theme here? There are a lot of fears we have felt, have dealt with, have faced head on, and are still struggling with. We can't write about this stuff without living it. We're sure you can add many more fears you have stressed about at one time or another as a pastor's wife, and so can we.

FROM ROBIN:

As our children got married and started to have children, they felt the pull to be themselves and not Robin and Jerry's son or daughter for once. Our sons and daughter wanted to make Kingdom changes on their own. Jerry and I had grown accustomed to them working alongside us in ministry, and they were our support group. Our kids were the ones I could always count on to be with me no matter what.

So when each of them started getting job opportunities and moving to other cities these changes surfaced a fear in me of doing ministry without my kids. It wasn't my kid's fault, I raised them their whole lives for the day they took flight. I had become comfortable with them being a part of our journey and ministry.

The Lord reminded me my only real attachment is Him. He told me I couldn't get comfortable with the people I was using as crutches because He would remove them. God didn't do this to hurt us; I think it was more about a health issue. At times we rely on them instead of on God. Or maybe my children were relying on us too much, and God wanted to grow them up as well. God pushes us to spread our wings at times, and spreading our wings is a fearful situation. This life with God is not about what makes us comfortable; it's about what makes us better.

God took a crutch of Robin's and removed it. She didn't want her children to leave her, but through this process of removal, God was able to show her the benefits of her children's independence, as well as a healthier relationship with Him. She watched as God also developed in her children a deeper connection to Him as they relied completely on God instead of mom and dad. What she feared, ended up being one of the greatest things that happened to her family.

Robin could have been like the hoarder who held on to her fears. She could have used everything in her power to make sure her children stayed in her town, at her church, involved in her and Jerry's ministry. But she faced her fears and bypassed island living.

I'm sure the men and women we see on these hoarding shows do not set out to become completely alone, having no visitors and repelling people by their lifestyle. This happens most often through a series of choices to hang on to fear instead of facing it head on.

When we hang on to our fears instead of allowing God to deal with them, we can picture packing them up to sail to the island. Every fear we allow to stay is one step closer to seclusion.

FROM SHEILA:

2015 was probably one of the toughest years we have ever had in ministry. We were seven years into our church plant when the doors miraculously opened for us to build on the property that had been donated to us. It was so exciting and pleasant the first few months, then the process began to take its toll. What started out as a big smile on my face soon turned to a worried strain. Through crooked contractors, construction crews not keeping their word, the costs being much higher than we were told, everything happening much slower than we had been promised, the excitement wore off quickly. I had many domestic and international travels that year, and my husband always likes to go with me as much as possible. I saw his mind be so wrapped up in the building that there were times he was drinking straight from the Pepto-Bismol bottle, sweating profusely for no reason, sleeping only sporadically in 1-2 hour intervals, talking on the phone from China for hours at a time, and wondering if the church would fire him after all of this was over. He was so stressed out that fear gripped my heart and mind.

I remember lying awake one night wondering if he was actually going to die during this process. I pictured my life without him and questioned if this building, this church, was worth it. I was gripped with fear for weeks, praying this process would soon be over.

No one knew the pressure we were living under during that year, and I felt very lonely and fearful. Not only might I lose my husband, but I might lose my church family and everything we worked for and loved. Fear became a way of life, so much so that I began to alter who I was to cope with and

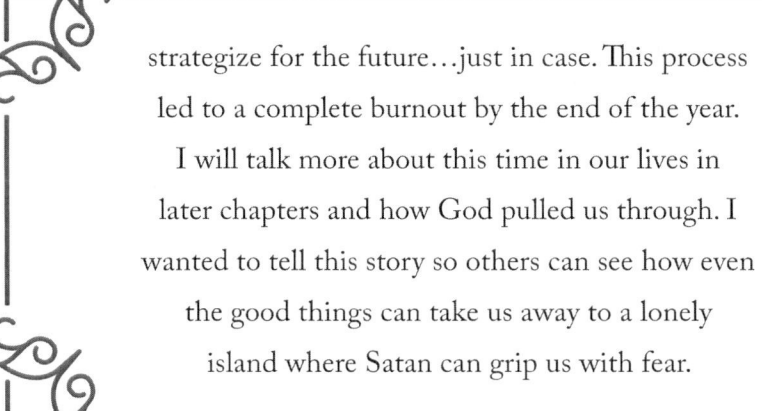

strategize for the future…just in case. This process led to a complete burnout by the end of the year. I will talk more about this time in our lives in later chapters and how God pulled us through. I wanted to tell this story so others can see how even the good things can take us away to a lonely island where Satan can grip us with fear.

The enemy stole much joy from Sheila during the building process. What should have been one of the happiest times in their lives, accomplishing one of the greatest feats they had ever undertaken, became saturated with fear and dread. She allowed circumstances she could see trump her faith in the God who brought them to this place. Fear won, and she can never have that time back.

Fear never has and never will come from the Lord. It's a proven fact that the majority of what we fear never happens. It is one of the strongest strategies the enemy uses to paralyze and discourage us. When you feel fear coming on, stop what you're doing and get in God's Word. Remind yourself of His promises and take all negative thoughts captive. (There's 2 Corinthians 10:5 again)

Just like the theme verse for this chapter says, "…God is with you wherever you go!" We added that exclamation point because that is a fact we can get excited about!

SELF-DEFENSE CAN WORK IN SPIRITUAL-DEFENSE

Sheila heard in a self-defense course one time that an attacker's number one weapon is surprise. He or she is counting on your fear to take advantage of you. The instructor taught that one of the greatest things you can do if you think you are being followed is to turn around and look right at the person.

That same thing works with the enemy. He is such a coward, and he is banking on your fear to take advantage of you. He knows your vulnerable spots, and ways to attack your mind. If fear starts creeping in, face it and speak directly to your perpetrator. Look him right in the face, and tell him he has no rights to you, your husband, your children, your future, your church, your livelihood, your family's health, or anything else you fear. God is with you wherever you go! Then start talking to the One who calms the storm and thank Him for your courage and backbone to stare fear down and walk the path He has planned for you.

FEAR

Several years ago we ran across this poem and it absolutely blew us away. Sheila held a women's conference in Nashville that year, and the theme was conquering fear. One of the pastor's wives quoted this monologue as a spoken word poem, and she did an incredible job. By the end, people were on their feet cheering and clapping. It came from *Propel Magazine*, a journal put out by Christine Caine and several others to help women find their potential in God. If you want to check them out further go to propelwomen.org Here is just a portion of the poem…Enjoy!

Fear has crippled many minds

Keeps the legs from walking

Running at full extension

Toward our goal toward our calling

This fear that causes our throats to close in keeps Our voices collapsing

until they're doomed to silence

Until we would rather not speak about injustice, Poverty, racism, abortion.

No one gets to the end of their life and thinks I wish I had been more scared.

Sometimes God soothes us,

But most of the time He does all He can to shake Some sense into us.

Maybe it's time we take our fears

And our hang-ups and give them up

For walking on water

For leaving the known for the unknown.

To take courage is to take heart

To take the very center of who we are

And risk it all for the good for the right for the very God who risked it

all to save our lives.

So, stand with shoulders back and feet planted firmly On faith ready to

act, pray, suffer, sacrifice, serve, love.

FROM ROBIN:

Want to know when fear hits me the hardest?

When I lay in bed at night, and I'm trying to sleep. Yep, when I need my rest the most, the enemy goes to work.

He tells me all sorts of things. If there are any challenging issues going on he wants me to fret and worry. Fear is a twin sister to worry, and the enemy uses it often.

I've learned to turn this fear on him. I use this very sentence when fear tries to rear its ugly head.

"Why is the enemy trying to bring fear into my life?" Why waste his time if nothing is going to happen? What is he afraid of? Fear tends to paralyze us and shut us down… so why is he using it on me? Here is what I've discovered. If we will seek God and let Him handle the concern, He will, but hear this. He will-His way, and in His timing. You know what? The enemy knows this as well. He is actually the one that is in fear.

Be encouraged today. If the enemy is trying to torment you while you sleep, turn it on him and pray. Soon he will get tired of you praying and try another tactic. Press in and trust God…and know help is on the way.

Trust is the key here. We can lean into a sovereign God who is keeping us, fighting for us, even when we cannot see it. He is bigger than any fear we face.

ANSWER & APPLY

1. What do I fear the most?

2. What percentage of my day does fear consume?

3. Do I see God helping me overcome this fear?

TAKEAWAY

Fear is like an ember dropped onto dry wood. If you don't stop fear, it will turn into a raging fire. God is bigger than any circumstance we face. He is not intimidated by any of them. It also helps to remember the enemy wouldn't use fear as a tactic unless he realized you would eventually succeed. God uses possibilities; where the enemy can only use probabilities.

"There are times when God's people suffer poisonous bites. However, sometimes they become so preoccupied with the bite until they fail to recognize they were not poisoned! What should have killed Paul did not harm him. What could have terminated Paul's life instead sparked an unexpected new chapter of ministry and divine favor in his life? The same can be true for every Christian."

Excerpt from *It's Not Punishment It's Preparation* by Augusta Reed

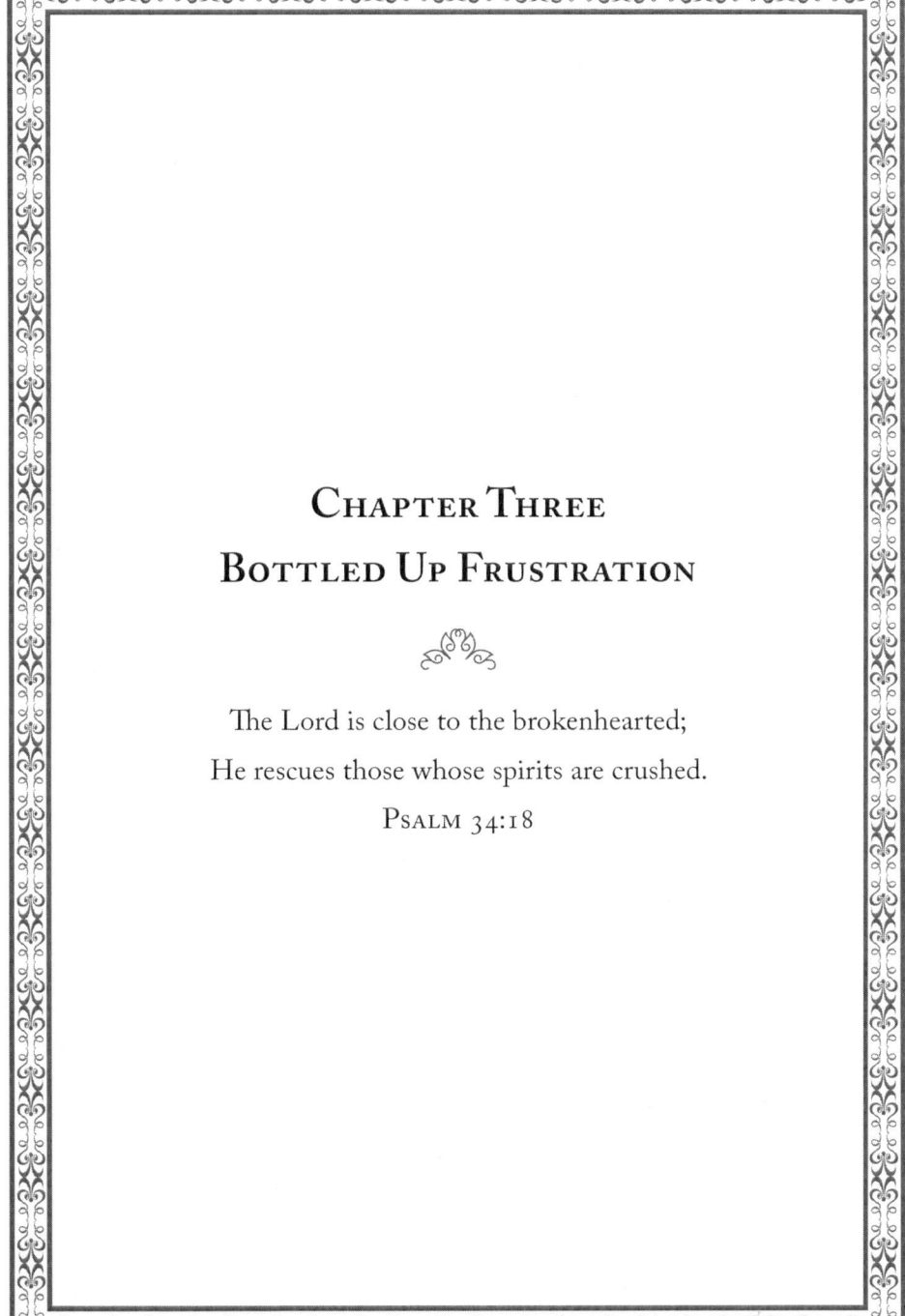

Chapter Three
Bottled Up Frustration

The Lord is close to the brokenhearted;
He rescues those whose spirits are crushed.
Psalm 34:18

We heard someone say that pastoring a church is like herding cats. I have to agree. Sometimes you just want to throw up your hands in frustration and not care.

FRUSTRATION = LOVE

Have you ever equated your frustration level with your care level? Why would you be frustrated about something if you cared nothing for it?

Pastors and their wives truly do care about the church family God has given them to shepherd. We have had the thought that, with the state of our world today, people have a hard time believing this is true.

I have not yet met a pastor or his wife who was in this business for the accolades, the easy living, the high salary, or the lack of stress. No, the pastors who are building their churches day in and day out are doing it because they love people. That love sometimes shows up in great frustration because we see people make choices that lead to really bad consequences. The families in our churches sometimes head in a direction we know is leading to destruction. We teach, we disciple, and we caution. And as they start down the wrong path we even want to run after them, but we know we must let them go.

These moments are especially tough when our church family does not ask for our blessing or counsel. You probably cannot count how many times these types of decisions have frustrated you in your congregation. This frustration often times can be turned into action, spilling outward and shaking those we love out of complacency. One time Sheila got so frustrated in a counseling session that she stood up and yelled some very hard truths to a couple. She was frustrated with their actions toward each other to the point of anger. Her actions, although unorthodox and not suggested, made the couple shred divorce papers right then.

Our frustration may be expressed toward our husbands, our children, and our church family, but we have to work through each one of these moments. We have to attempt to fix the problems around us, and if they are beyond our ability to fix, then we must learn to live with them without being overcome with their consequences. When we recognize our frustration comes from a place of love, care, and concern for others, then dealing with the problems becomes easier. Praying in spite of the frustration creates in us tender hearts and loving compassion.

FROM SHEILA:

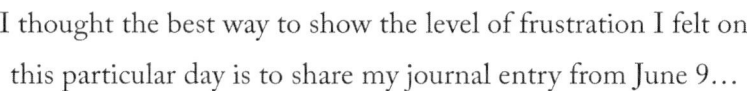

I thought the best way to show the level of frustration I felt on this particular day is to share my journal entry from June 9...

"Yesterday was a horrible day. We lost a family in the church that I thought were friends and would stay committed. They had just told us how they want their kids to grow up in this church. My heart is absolutely broken. I feel so sorry for my husband. I don't even know what to say. Lord, please heal our hearts quickly and show us what we need to do differently. I want to see Your hand in this. Just saying God's weeding out the unfaithful, or people telling us it's going to be okay is not enough. The only thing that matters is what YOU say. Could we experience some victory? Could we hear from You that this is worth it? Can we know what we're doing wrong? This has made me even question if we're in the right profession because it doesn't seem as though we're very good at this. I woke up thinking about a line from a song we sang Sunday, 'Let it go my soul and trust in Him. The waves and wind still know His name.' I've wasted so much time in fear, doubt, worry, sadness, frustration, and anger when all the time I could be living in the freedom Christ brings. I have to make a choice, Lord. I can let this pile up on me, or I can live free."

You can tell there was much pain in that journal entry. I felt betrayed, lied to, and let down in a huge way. Frustration was at an all-time high. I loved these people, and I felt like they had made a gradual fade away from the things of God. Then they pulled the "God" card saying God told them to leave our church. What do you say to that? You don't want to be so arrogant as to tell them God didn't tell them such a thing. Maybe God did tell them, but in my experience, the people who are blessed going out, are the ones who do it openly and go to something greater, not those who hide behind a façade of lies.

It's easy to say that out of all the pastor's wives we talk to, people leaving the church this way has to be one of the largest frustrations we face. This frustration comes because we love the people, we love those who are attached to the family leaving, and we love our church.

TOO LEGIT TO QUIT

Our frustrations as pastors' wives are legitimate. These difficulties can be the catalyst that keeps us going. These irritations we face on a regular basis can be the very thing that drives us to do more, love more, and protect our church families more. If we allow them to become a positive counterweight they keep us going, preventing us from quitting our purpose. Instead of these frustrations sailing us to the island, we can transform them into the very platform we stand on.

FROM ROBIN:

Our church was on a 21-day Daniel fast. During this time, we opened the church every night for 2 hours to pray. So many times, we opened the church 20 min early and left late. Many nights I would sit in the church and wonder, "Where are my elders? Where are my leaders? Can they not just come for 10 min?"

I would think about a person's marriage that I knew was falling apart or another family's child who was gone for over a year, and they can't even show up for 10 minutes to pray? I know what they're going through. They have an opportunity to reach the throne room, and they pass it up. I was extremely frustrated that our leaders didn't take this time more seriously.

There is something sacrificially powerful about getting out of our comfy clothes to drive to the church in the rain. God sees those moments when we press through and make our way to Him. He notices, and He blesses these actions. These moments that seem as though others have a lack of care or sense of urgency produce frustration. If we don't watch it, these annoyances can make us cross over into anger.

We know we have allowed anger to set in when the same people who will not participate in prayer, or other activities at the church, come to us and lay out all their prayer needs before us. They want us to pray for the very things they were not willing to sacrifice their time to pray for. When anger toward these things shows up, then we know we have crossed over into an area that is not pleasing to God. There is a fine line between stewardship and ownership. We have to remember we are stewards, not owners. And when we cross over into ownership we can easily become judgmental.

We believe the anger comes from a place of love, but we're also hurt over their desire to sacrifice our time above their own. Deep down what we really want is for people to just be hungry and have a passion to serve God. Praying for the needs of others is what we do! These prayers are easier to accomplish when we know they are united with the person needing prayer.

COUNSELING 101

Another form of frustration we often face is when we counsel someone, and the counselee does not take our advice. Their situation may continually worsen during our counseling, but they don't change their behavior. Many times, they blame the church, or worse, they blame you for nothing changing. You may want to just cut them loose and say forget it, but that action is not the answer. Our frustration is born out of love and concern for that person, so allow your frustration to be used in a positive way. Going the distance with someone may be the answer, but often times we may need to assess when it's appropriate to refer someone to a Christian, professional counselor.

Love is the catalyst for our feelings of frustration. We entered the ministry with other people in mind. Our words and actions are almost always about other people. These same people aren't always spending their words and actions to be about us, and that's okay. We have to remember, we are the ones in ministry, and stop expecting others to respond the way we would in certain situations.

Often times, we have an expectation that our congregation is going to act like we would act. That is a wrong belief to have. If we continue having this expectation it leads to great frustration. If we do not harness our frustration it turns to anger. This anger can lead to a belief that all people are going to treat us wrongly because they didn't live up to our expectations. This belief pushes us to pack our bags and head off to the island.

We have to move forward fulfilling the expectation God has for us as His children, utilizing our God-given gifts and talents. Each of us, as individuals, has a calling from God to complete certain tasks. He gave us all different gifts and talents. Those gifts and talents are to help us build His Kingdom with beautiful souls He places in front of us. If we are being the best version of us we can be, then God will take care of the rest of the story.

CHURCH GROWTH-FRUSTRATION FOR DAYS

I can guarantee very few of us believe our churches are growing at the rate we dreamed or believed they would. We hear about so-and-so who planted a church last year, and they're now running 8,000 people. If we allow ourselves to play the comparison game those stories can make some swell with pride and others feel like failures.

Comparison is our enemy. Comparison leads to frustration, feelings of failure, and pride. I've never compared myself to someone who can make me feel good about being average. Comparing our calling to someone else's will do the same thing. It will puff us up with pride or make us believe we're a dismal failure, both of which keep us in a state of perpetual frustration.

If we look around at the job we are doing in our churches, and it is the best we can possibly accomplish, then we have to be happy with the blessings God is releasing to our church. At the same time, if we take an honest look at the job we are doing and find lack, we must change our actions immediately. Lives are at stake. Don't live with the frustration of a less than adequate job performance.

Many times, as the pastor's wife, you are not in charge. You may be on your church staff or have another job entirely outside the church. Whatever your situation, we have the potential to see things that are wrong in our churches. This can lead to frustration as well. These irritations may come because our husbands might not be taking care of the situation as we would. Listen ladies, there is nothing more the enemy would love than to separate and divide you and your husband. There is nothing that will wreck a church quicker than a pastor's marriage divided.

There is a reason why your husband is the lead pastor and you are not. We can guarantee God knew what He was getting into when He called your husband to lead. Instead of fighting your husband, take him by the hand and lock arms with him. Celebrate the ministry wins with your husband. Help him where he needs help, pray for him in areas he is lacking, and then shut your mouth.

Yes, We Said Shut Your Mouth

Often times, we are derailing our husband's calling because we are griping about everything. What we do not see is that we are emasculating our husbands, irritating him to no end, making him lose confidence in his abilities, and the whole church suffers because of it.

Go read Proverbs 27:15. No, seriously we meant that. Go read it right now. Do you want to be known as THAT wife? Seriously…think about the words you are saying to your husband. He may be a very frustrating man, and we understand that. But speak to the man you want him to become. Stop speaking to the man you believe he is right now. Close your mouth, pray for what you see needs to change, and then speak words of confidence, life, promotion, power, and belief into his life.

We challenge you also to pray for yourself and ask God to show you what YOU need to change so the church can move forward. Make sure you are not the source of frustration. That is a very scary prayer to pray, but when you do, be willing to change whatever God tells you needs to be changed.

Trapped

You may have already tried all we are encouraging you to try in this chapter. You may feel as though you are trapped in this perpetual state of frustration because nothing is budging in your life. God doesn't even relate to the word trapped. If He has you in a place or situation He is doing something behind the scenes that you may not be able to see. Listen to what we're about to say. I mean truly listen and let these words sink in deeply because there are no truer words ever spoken than God's Word.

What you are doing is one of the hardest jobs anyone has ever done. The reward is great, and much is at stake, that's why it is so hard. You may feel trapped, but you have to decide sooner or later that either God is God or He's not. Do you trust Him with your life or not? Do you believe He can turn all this frustration to good?

Check out Romans 8:28 for instance. These are not trite sayings. They are the truth, and you have to decide which way you will turn. Will you stand firm or let the hard part of this job win? It's up to you whether or not you stay on the island.

And we know that God causes everything to work together for the good of those who love God and are called according to His purpose for them. Romans 8:28

If we truly believe what Romans 8:28 says then we have no other choice than to press in and wait with great expectancy to see what God is doing in our situation.

ANSWER & APPLY

1. What is the root of my frustration?

2. Do I find my frustration bleeding over into other areas of my life?

3. Is frustration about to wreck my life?

4. How can God help me overcome this frustration?

Takeaway

Find someone you can talk to about your frustrations. There are times you just need a trusted friend, your spouse, or a counselor to help you process what you are feeling. Also, listening to podcasts are always good to get someone else's perspective, especially when you are struggling with frustration.

Chapter Four

Sad Sundays

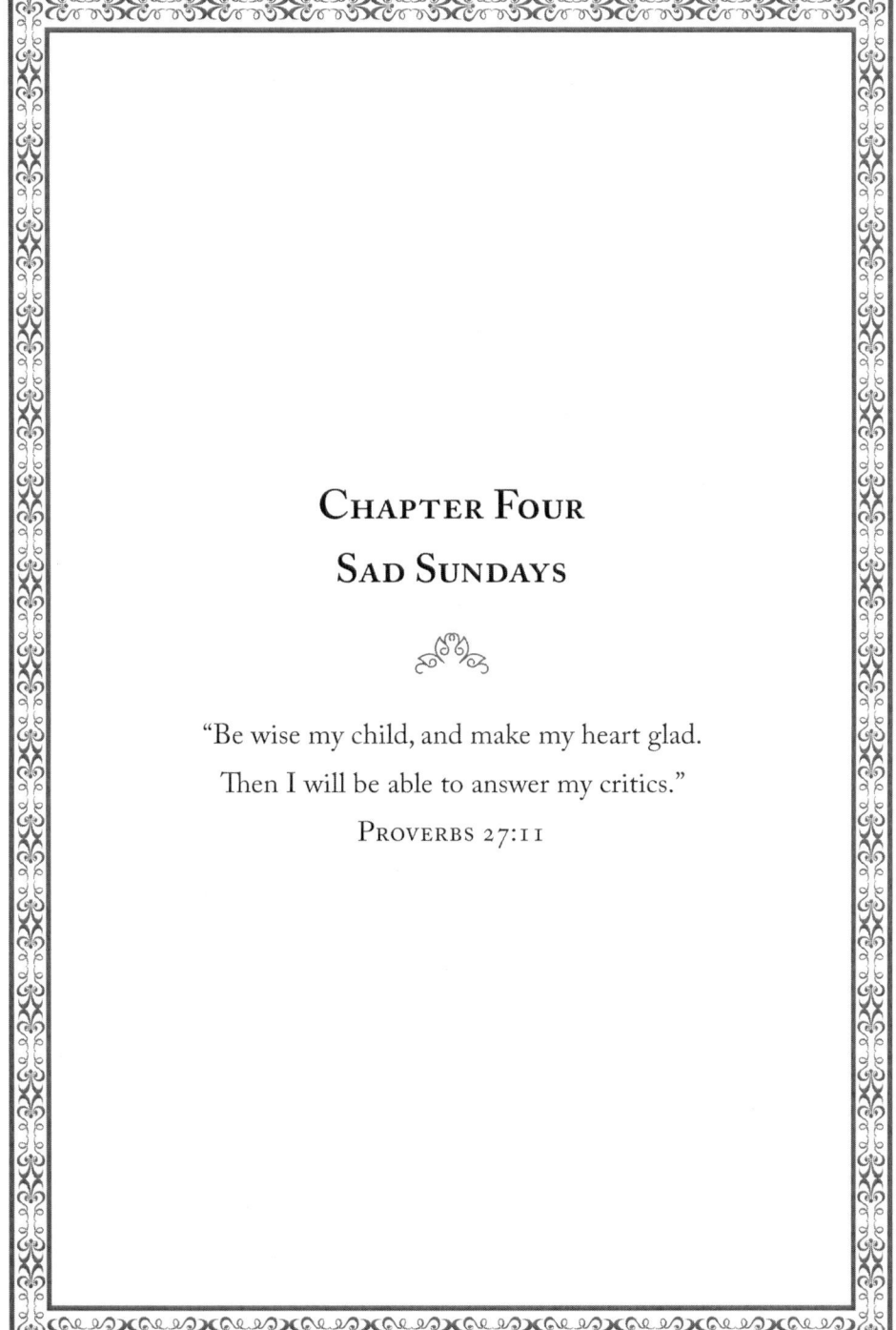

"Be wise my child, and make my heart glad.

Then I will be able to answer my critics."

Proverbs 27:11

There are many reasons why Sundays can be sad for some of us. As pastors' wives, we have endured many sad Sundays. We have all seen the posts from our optimistic friends who post almost every church day, "THIS IS THE DAY THE LORD HAS MADE WE SHALL REJ"----WHAT??? If this is a day the Lord has made, then why am I not rejoicing, and why am I not glad? Can anybody relate?

It's not that we don't enjoy going to church, it's just that sometimes these Sundays are hard and we would rather stay in bed. Getting up to face critics, or defend your husband, or whatever makes you sad, is just more, at times, than we have psyched ourselves out for. Having a sad Sunday is enough to make you want to sail away on the island and live in seclusion.

Words Do Hurt

We were taught as children that sticks and stones break our bones, but words do not harm us. Then we learn as adults nothing is further from the truth. Words are powerful weapons. Words are sometimes meant to harm, destroy, or derail us. The enemy can orchestrate the words of others to stop us from building God's Kingdom. Words have split churches, ended marriages, destroyed friendships, and caused irreparable harm. God's Word tells us in Proverbs 18:21 that the tongue can bring forth life and death.

When we have been repeatedly criticized, or we've had to listen to criticism about our spouse or children, going to church with the critics becomes a chore some days.

CRITICISM...

Our shepherd is also our husband. When we're hurt, and our shepherd doesn't do what we expected, then that puts us on an island. We may believe or even know that if hurtful words had been spoken to anyone else he would have protected that person.

Our husbands are in a precarious situation. He may be trying to navigate difficult waters. He may not know if he should react as a husband or a shepherd. If he reacts as a husband it may be too strong because the church member is looking at him as a shepherd. If he reacts as a shepherd, you may be mad because he wasn't strong enough. If this is your situation, it may be that your husband was completely and totally wrong in how he handled a criticism or incident involving you. If that is the case, then you must dust yourself off, pick up the pieces, and move on. Forgive him, and make sure you discuss how this has affected you. The enemy would love for you and your husband to be divided. Division is one of his powerful schemes. Forgiveness of the offense toward your husband makes you conquer-proof, and conquer-proof will keep you island-living-proof.

POINTED CRITICISMS
ARE THE WORST

There is another form of criticism we have to deal with quite often in the church; church members who want to tell you what your husband is doing wrong so you can "fix him".

These criticisms may come masked as false concern or a joke as the person laughingly delivers the harsh words. You may be the only one in the circle who knows the back-story and knows they truly mean the comment as a cruel criticism. What's even worse is they may be saying the very thing you have to deal with at home! He or she may be calling out the very hot spot that causes arguments in your family. That moment feels as though they are airing your dirty laundry right there in front of whoever is near and listening.

Those words cause us damage. Not only do they validate the pains you feel in your marriage, but they cause embarrassment because you know the criticism is based on fact. The minute we agree with the critic who is sticking their head into our business, we've lost. It is in those moments your husband has to know you have his back. Both our husbands and we, as pastors' wives, have to protect and watch out for our spouses. When the time comes for you to go to your next assignment, whether it's retirement or another church, you have to know above all else you can count on each other.

Keep those issues at home when it comes to disparaging comments. Stand united against those critics and never let them get the best of you, your husband, or your church. They have no right to drive you to an island of fear and doubt about your husband. Stay unified in those moments, and you will always come out better.

A Great Read

Warren D. Bullock in his book, *When Words Hurt* says, "Religious people are in the business of endeavoring to be good. They are therefore tempted to point out the faults of others, so that by implication they themselves may appear better. It is a miserable business."

When people start to see the cracks in your husband's armor it may lead to criticism. He still needs to see and hear your respect and belief in him. Remember we are speaking to the man we want him to be! We know how hard he works, how much he loves people, and what's going on behind the scenes. We live with him. We witness the sleepless nights and continued prayer for people. The church family has one shepherd to watch, but he has hundreds, sometimes thousands of people he's trying to keep up with. It's not easy!

IGNORANCE

How many times have critics turned on you when they didn't know all the details? How many times have you been tempted to share openly all the details of another person's failure? We know…it's tempting to just throw the person who is causing the rift under the bus. But we implore you…DON'T GO THERE! You're better than that, you're wiser than that, you're classier than that!

Often times the person criticizing thinks they know the full story, but they do not. They see a decision your husband made in the church, they believe it was wrong, so they make sure everyone knows their opinion. Such people are reacting out of total ignorance to the situation. They were not in the meetings. They are not aware of all the phone calls, emails, and striving your husband may have gone through before making the decision. You can simply overlook those critics. Sure, they may hurt you; they may even turn people away from the church, but their influence is temporary. God has a way of exposing people who come against His Church.

In Exodus 23:6 God tells us to never charge anyone falsely with evil. When people do that very thing to us, He will do our defending. God is not playing when it comes to false charges being waged against His anointed.

There will be times when criticism will devastate you. In those moments, there is also an opportunity to grow stronger. Use these moments to learn how to not let the words affect you as deeply. Take thoughts captive.

Bring those thoughts before Jesus and let Jesus formulate your next words or actions. Robin says, "It helps me to remember the Lord was perfect, and still He was rejected and criticized." Why would we think we should be exempt from the same treatment? It's part of being a leader. It's also in times like these God gives you supernatural wisdom to handle the attack. He uses this time to sharpen and develop in us the leader He called us to be. God doesn't waste any situation. He has great lessons for us to learn in every one of them.

Blessed Are The Peacemakers

If we do not swim out to the island, the Lord can use these times to grow our reliance on Him and bring the happy back into Sundays. These difficult moments are also an opportunity to build relationships with the offending people. If you are feeling a rift between you and the other person, set an appointment, take the time to hear them out, and ask for forgiveness if warranted. Leadership is hard, and it challenges us to take the high road. If possible try to correct the issue before it grows out of control.

The greatest way to do this is by keeping the circle small. By that, we mean try to do your part in keeping the offense between the two of you. Use the Matthew 18 principle of going to that person and talking openly to work things out. Anytime I have personally had to do this or counseled someone else to enact this standard, the relationship has been strengthened. We must go into the meeting, not with the attitude of proving we are right, but instead with the attitude of restoring the relationship. When we set love and restoration as the precedent, the other person sees and hears our heart. Soft answers really do turn away wrath!

Is The Bathroom Door Your Friend?

Often times, Sunday's make us want to escape. Our bodies are present at church, but instead of embracing the moment, we search for escape routes. We avoid, deflect, and run when God can give us the strength to stand strong. If you need to, take a time out occasionally, but then jump right back in.

From Sheila:

Not long after we started the church, we had people who made me feel rejected, betrayed, and alone. They left us after proclaiming to stay with us and help us build this church. Some would leave offended making us feel as though we were terrible people. Others left and told complete falsehoods about their time at our church, making others believe we were doing a really bad job. It was tough, to say the least. I thought this church was going to be a simple continuation of success we had experienced before.

Every Sunday I would walk into church with butterflies in my stomach, full of dread for who was not there, who had left, who was going to say something mean, and who was going to complain. I would make it in the door, but then after greeting a few people, I would make my way to the bathroom. It was one room and a complete solace from the crowd. I would go in there, lean on the back of the door, and fight tears. I loved those few minutes of solitude away from the staring eyes.

Feeling lonely in a crowd is nothing new. We have a tendency to escape when these times come to us. Your way of escape may look different from Sheila's but still, it's an escape instead of healthy interaction.

Escape is necessary, and there is nothing wrong with removing yourself from the fray from time to time. But closing yourself off from interaction and believing the lies that no one loves you, makes you vulnerable to island living.

FROM ROBIN:

The enemy is always trying to divide us from the Life Source we need which is God and others. I went through a season where we were being accused of things that were not true. It made me feel very suspicious of people and their motives. I found myself drawing away from everything and those that loved me dearly. I felt very alone.

Ministry is challenging in that we know a lot we cannot share. This often puts us on the island the book is talking about. But God showed me through His patience and understanding that rejection, offense, and suffering is all part of the plan. As we draw closer to Him our anointing grows. So the opposition does, as well. No matter where you do ministry know this, pain will follow, but God will grow in you the very things you need to overcome and become the leader He designed you to be. With every assignment comes adversity, but take this as a good sign. It's time to squash the victim mentality and realize the enemy is aware of your potential.

Being treated this way can cause a lot of sad Sundays. These moments can make you question whether or not anyone cares at all.

Believing these kinds of lies can drive you straight to the island with a guarded heart and a 10-foot electric fence surrounding you. You do not have to go there.

Facebook: Friend or Foe

We were never de-friended on Facebook until we became lead pastors' wives. We had some of these friends for years and never once did we get de-friended. What's up with that??

How many of us have seen derogatory comments about ourselves, our husbands, or our kids personally on Facebook? Man, that really stinks when that happens. Then you're left with the aftermath, the pieces of a broken heart, even a raging heart full of anger!

You are then expected to show up on Sunday and not want to punch someone in the throat. These are surreal moments that make you believe you are expected not to feel, not to hurt, and not to have regular girl emotions. It seems you're expected to show up with your church smile and love everybody.

Take Robin's advice, and do a little thing she likes to call, "Fasting the Feed". If Facebook starts to get you down, then fast the newsfeed. Use Facebook as a place to post encouragement. Only get on long enough to tell other people who are reading your stuff how great God is, what He's done in your life, and how they can have Him too. Turn Facebook into an open letter you write to your friends letting them all know of Christ's love.

The truth is, when we start living for others' applause and approval we move to the island. We become this plastic, shallow version of ourselves always pleasing others instead of pleasing the One who sent us, created us, and is giving us the strength to do this job. We have to remember in those moments we have an audience of ONE. One ladies…ONE!

He is cheering you on. He believes in you. He is not criticizing you or telling you to act a certain way, dress a certain way, or love a certain way. He simply wants you to seek holiness, and when we are pursuing Him, the rest takes care of itself. His burden is light. His yoke is easy. We're never going to please everyone. When we try to do this, the burden becomes unbearable, and the yoke is too much for us to carry. This happens when we assume the expectations of others we were never asked to take on.

We are nothing without Him. So fill yourself to the brim with His love, His patience, His endurance, and let that spill out all over everybody. Stop relying on your own strength to run this race. His strength never runs out or gets tired.

The man or woman in front of you is God's child, and you have been given the opportunity to love them and be obedient to God. If they refuse to pick up what you're laying down that's their decision, but you will know you did what was right before God.

The Blame Game

Sometimes, no matter what biblical steps we take it just does not work. Some people will always have an excuse. They will always find ways to justify their behavior or offense. I heard a very wise pastor say once, "If people are always finding fault with you, they don't have to find fault in themselves."

Blaming others has caused many a sad Sunday. Playing the blame game pits spouse against spouse, and church family against each other. The wife and husband then blame each other, the church blames us, and we blame the church. The blamer/critic will always believe there is something wrong with the church, instead of giving the church the benefit of the doubt. The church is supposed to be a family. Do you just get up and leave your family when you have a disagreement or dispute? What happened to working it out?

When a person can blame someone else for things not happening as they anticipated, then they never have to take responsibility. Many times, they pull the "God card" and say God is telling them to leave their church family. This stabs at rejection and hurts those who have gone the distance with them. No one wins in the blame game. Never get caught up in this game. Let it stop with you by taking responsibility for what you need to, and bringing peace to other situations.

ANSWER & APPLY

1. Do I dread weekends?

2. The closer it gets to Sunday; how do I feel?

3. When you walk through the church doors, are you looking forward to or dreading what's about to happen?

4. What steps do I need to take to not dread Sundays?

TAKEAWAY

Unity is one of the most powerful gifts given to man. We were called to be peacemakers and grace-givers. When being blamed or criticized find a kind and loving way to soothe the hurting person and help them resolve their issues. Remember… "Blessed are the peacemakers for they shall be called children of God." Matthew 5:9

"As Christians undergo periods of preparation they encounter various odds, situations, or times when they are met with opposition. These odds may affect numerous areas of their lives. They may find themselves feeling weary, disgusted, and discouraged. Nonetheless, when they know this opposition is not punishment, but preparation, they will not lose heart. They will not throw in the towel. They will not buckle under the pressure."

Excerpt from *It's Not Punishment It's Preparation* by Augusta Reed

CHAPTER FIVE
GLASS HOUSES

But the Lord said, "Don't judge by his appearance or
height, for I have rejected him. The Lord doesn't see
things the way you see them. People judge by
outward appearance, but the Lord looks at the heart".

1 SAMUEL 16:7

When we talk about glass houses, we're not talking about a small town in England or an album by Billy Joel. We didn't even know these two things existed until we asked Siri and Google about glass houses. We were curious to find what the world was saying about this ambiguous subject.

The saying goes, "People who live in glass houses shouldn't throw stones." Well, we're saying people who live in glass houses shouldn't have the stinkin' stones thrown at them! Our definition of glass houses is the way in which we live as pastors' wives feeling as though our entire lives are constantly on display.

When a person lives with the strain of their children's behavior being critiqued, or the cleanliness of her home constantly examined, or the car she drives annoyingly analyzed, etc. etc. then the feeling of glass house living sets in. Before we know it we're trying to live up to everyone else's expectations, keeping up appearances instead of truly living.

This belief that it is acceptable for us to live in glass houses as pastors' wives is the reason we chose the verse at the beginning of this chapter. We need to be reminded what our Creator looks at when it comes to judging us. Our hearts.

Man does look at the outward appearance. As pastors' wives, we will always be subject to the same scrutiny; this is a fact that will never go away. We cannot, should not, and will not rely on man's opinion for our worth or our identity. Repeat after me…I cannot, should not, and will not rely on man's opinion for my worth or my identity.

God's opinion of my heart is all that matters. Certainly, we must maintain civility and live life so that accusations toward us are viewed as ridiculous, but we cannot let others drive our attitudes or actions.

FROM ROBIN:

I grew up in a pastor's home so all I knew was this concept of glass house living. "People are always watching how you respond to things," my mother would tell me. "It matters how you act, and you want to represent Christ well." I was blessed with the most amazing parents in the world. They actually lived what they taught, and they really showed me that above everything else it matters what God thinks.

I had to wear skirts all the time, no pants because the pastor's kid was not allowed to wear such things. I also wanted to be a cheerleader, and that was taboo. If I wanted to go to a sleepover where a boy was in the family I was not allowed because of the way it looked. I wasn't allowed to wear jewelry or anything like that. I had a hideous shell necklace that I would hide in my pocket and put on at school just because I could. I was such a rebel...

I was finally allowed to try out for the basketball team. Making the team was a huge victory for me. Our team went to the state tournament, and I was named MVP. My time on the basketball team did not come without some tough moments. The girls all played in shorts, and I begged my mom to allow me to wear shorts too. She was cool with it, but I was under so much pressure to keep up appearances that she decided to make my shorts for me. Imagine my excitement. So here I would go in my felt shorts that came all the way down to my knees, except I would roll them up as high as they could go and pin them. The cuff would be 2 inches thick, but I was trying my hardest to fit in. They would droop between the pins and looked horrible. It's hilarious now, but back then there was a lot of pressure from living in a glass house.

GLASS HOUSE ASSESSMENT

Robin said it perfectly when she called this way of living "pressure". Who can keep up those types of appearances and not be traumatized? Felt shorts? That's a trauma all in itself!

Seriously though, it's time to take an assessment of the level of glass house living you are doing. Let's find the places we can remove the pressure from our lives.

1. Do you keep the blinds drawn all day so no one can see in? In other words, do you keep a guard around your heart and words and emotions with others so they do not see anything personal?

2. Do you dress your children for others to approve?

3. Do you work tirelessly to keep your house clean "in case a church member drops by?"

nts with no make-up on. There is a level of familiarity that shouldn't be hed.

    People should know they can call on you to come and pray with them e hospital, make those midnight runs for their sick kid, and all the other ents of crisis we get called for. Those moments are an unbelievable privi-to be allowed into others' lives. Very few people have that privilege, but you pastor's wife get it often.

THOSE PEOPLE

    Glass house living puts what Sheila's husband Jack calls, "The spirit tupid" on some people. We asked some of our pastor's wife friends if they ever had someone say something unbelievable to them. You know that ment when you're left with your mouth gaping open trying to decide if they ly meant what you think they meant by their statement. Below are some of ir responses... with a few of our dreamed-up replies. I'm sure you could add ir own 2 or 3 or 25 to the list!

"Oh, is this your mom?"
While sitting with someone 2 years younger

"You look so much older!"
After losing 20 lbs.

"Isn't this the 3rd new pair of shoes you're wearing this month?"
Really? They counted???

"You're missing too much church!"
After missing our 5th Sunday IN SEVEN YEARS

4. If a church member gets in your car do you make s   ma
   tuned to the local Christian station so they won't kı   brea
   listen to and love 70's rock?

5. Do you hide expensive jewelry or clothing and only
   away from church members?

These are just some of the questions to ask yourself and
thinking about where you allow the pressure from glass house
trate your family's lives.

He Knew What
He Was Getting Into

When God called you into leadership He knew you ha
that you may not have recognized in yourself. He equipped you
gifts to accomplish your calling. Now that being said, people are w
at all times. Is it fair? No, but Kingdom work isn't always fair. Our v
results rarely turn out like we think it will.

We have to please God before we please man. Because we
ple are watching what we do, it is important to be a good example
sent Christ well. But at the same time, we cannot lose who we truly
process.

Being in a small-town Robin can't go anywhere without peoj
ing who she and Jerry are, watching what they do, and how they
There is a mantle that we all wear (which we'll talk about later in t
that deserves the dignity, honor, and respect afforded to a pastor and
But there's also that part of us that just wants to run to Wal-Mart in c

"You've put on a lot of weight lately"

"I hope you don't mind but I have a crush on your husband"
And I'm supposed to be okay with this...why???

"Wow. You finally did your hair!"
Well, the wolves who raised me finally gave me permission.

After being at the hospital all night with their son who was in a horrific car crash, his emergency surgery was finally scheduled for 1:00 pm the next day, a Sunday. A guest speaker spoke for obvious reasons. A church member visited them during the surgery and said...

"You guys could have come to church then since
the surgery was scheduled for 1 o'clock."

"Does your 14-year-old daughter have migraines because of secret sin in her life?"

"I know when God speaks to me because it
sounds just like your husband's voice."
God...my husband...same thing...

"Did you ever think to pray for her healing?"
Speaking of very sick pastor's daughter.

"What do you do all day?"
I just sit and read my Bible...that's it...just sit and read my Bible.

"What do you look like when you don't have
makeup on and your hair is messed up?"

This pastor's wife walked into church in her new outfit feeling really beautiful,

"Wow! You've gained weight, but that looks good on you."

This one is the coup de gras of all statements…After coming off sabbatical
a man at church walked up, jiggled this pastor's wife's belly and said,

"I thought you were going to be fasting."

ANSWER & APPLY

1. Do I resent my position?

2. Do I withhold my true emotions because of what others might think?

3. Do I believe others are waiting for me to make a mistake?

4. What is one scripture that reminds me who I am in Christ?

And with that, we close this chapter with a good reminder for all of us.

TAKEAWAY

When God calls you to lead, He calls others to follow, and in the following,
they are watching. Let this be an opportunity to show them grace and mercy.
Remember most people have no idea the challenges you face. They don't see
the expectations as unreasonable. It's always good to shake it off and ask yourself this question: *Is God pleased with my reactions and my inner thoughts?* At the
end of the day what He thinks is all that really matters.

"People who choose to remain as islands miss their greater purpose in God's Kingdom and they rob the rest of the body of linking arms, leaving holes of vulnerability within the ranks. The enemy, then, has easier access to wound and distract fellow soldiers."

Deborah Stricklin from *In The Stillness*

PART TWO:
COMING OUT OF ISLAND LIVING

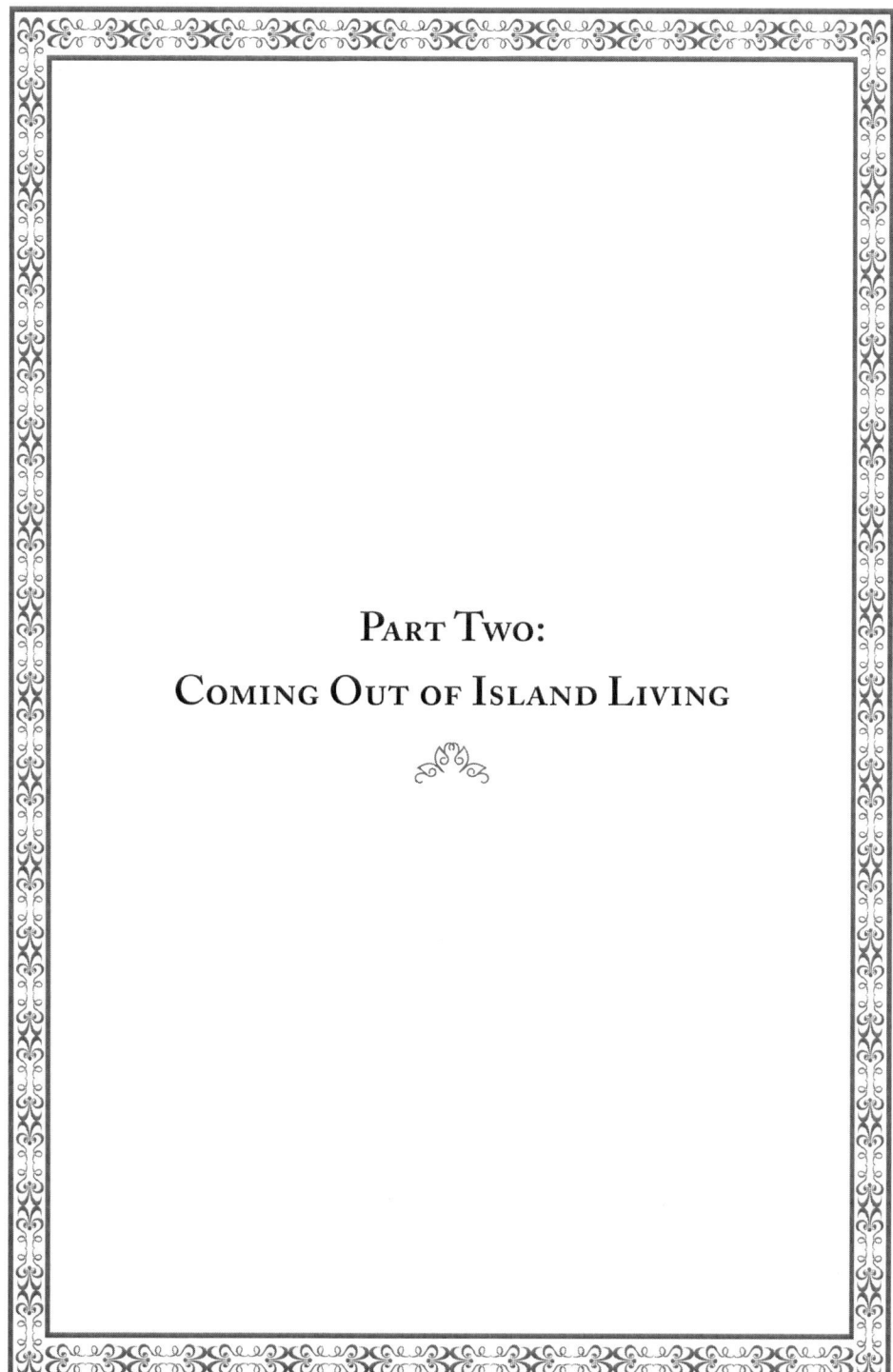

Joseph… Oh, how we admire him for his tenacity and strength. The scriptures never tell us he got bitter or had unforgiveness in his heart because of the mistreatment by his brothers. His story in Genesis is quite fascinating. This tale starts with a dream and ends with Joseph being Pharaoh's right-hand man. But much happens in between. His brothers are jealous so they throw him in a pit; then traders sell him for money. He ends up in Potiphar's house and is accused of trying to rape Potiphar's wife. Potiphar becomes enraged and throws him in prison. While in prison he meets Pharaoh's chief butler and chief baker. They have dreams, and he interprets these dreams. He tells them to remember him when they are released, but they forget. One day Pharaoh has a dream, and the chief butler then remembers Joseph and tells Pharaoh about him. Joseph is then released and brought to Pharaoh to explain what his dreams mean, and the rest is history. All the promises God had given him finally came, and the struggles that made no sense at the time were the very struggles that made him the leader God wanted him to be.

Just like us, Joseph could have lost hope, which I'm sure at times he did. He had a heavy mantle to carry but God equipped him through his struggles to wear the mantle well. God was preparing Joseph for greater things, through every trial he faced. The expectations for Joseph proved to be extremely hard. But God helped him every step of the way. Just like God's plans for Joseph, He has big plans for you. Joseph could have removed himself from people and protected his heart and mind from further hurt. If he had, he would have missed out on seeing his entire family restored and his dreams come true.

Don't let the mess of ministry keep you from the mission of ministry. It's time to find your way back. It's time to get back on dry land.

"The devil on his best day didn't destroy you on your worst day."

~ Christine Caine ~

CHAPTER SIX
MINDING THE MANTLE

When they came to the other side, Elijah said to Elisha,
"Tell me what I can do for you before I am taken away."
And Elisha replied, "Please let me inherit a double share
of your spirit and become your successor." "You have
asked a difficult thing," Elijah replied. "If you see me when I am
taken from you, then you will get your request. But if not,
then you won't." As they were walking along and talking,
suddenly a chariot of fire appeared, drawn by horses of fire.
It drove between the two men, separating them, and Elijah was
carried by a whirlwind into heaven. Elisha saw it and cried
out, "My father! My father! I see the chariots and
charioteers of Israel!" And as they disappeared from sight,
Elisha tore his clothes in distress. Elisha picked up
Elijah's cloak, which had fallen when he was taken up.
Then Elisha returned to the bank of the Jordan River.

2 KINGS 2:9-13

Don't worry, we're not going to ask you to memorize that whole section. We just wanted you to get a feel for the events taking place here. You may feel a lot like Elisha in this story. You were just walking along when suddenly a chariot of fire and a whirlwind came through, and everything shifted. Now here you are a pastor's wife. And just like Elisha, you may have been mentored and led by the best example around…or maybe not. Either way, we really don't feel as though there is adequate preparation to take on this mantle (aka the awesome, honored, yet sometimes overwhelming leadership position you hold as a pastor's wife) until you are smack dab in the middle of all that is happening. One day you look up brow beaten, war-torn, scarred, and realize this is a whole new ballgame. This is a mantle you have been given to wear and it is truly a privilege to have.

Make It A Double Please

Elisha asked for the mantle, but there were certain prerequisites that had to be met first. We can see there are definite steps he had to take to be able to inherit the mantle of a double portion of Elijah's anointing. He took those steps, and then what does it say he did? He fell down, screaming, and ripped his clothes in deep distress. In other words, he got exactly what he asked for; so why was he in distress? Why did he tear his clothes? Why did he yell? Shouldn't the ending of the story go something like this?

Then God answered Elisha's wish, and because of that Elisha fell down in deep, humble gratitude thanking God all the days of his life. He then skipped off doing a happy dance with music playing in the background and lived happily ever after.

Okay, well, maybe that isn't how the story went, but isn't that what we expect sometimes in our own lives? We get what we asked for, what we feel God is calling us to, then when we realize it's too stressful, we fall down yelling at God and tearing our clothes. In today's world, it would be better described as…we cry and whine to our husbands, we harbor unforgiveness and blame for the people who have hurt us, and we isolate ourselves to protect our hearts.

This can no longer be.

We don't believe Elisha was in distress for the same reasons we are sometimes in distress, but he certainly must have felt the weight of what he was carrying. This mantle that was just handed to him was something he desired, but he knew it would come with a price. He must have felt the price immediately realizing his mentor and friend was gone, and now he was all alone.

What does this passage of scripture say Elisha did after this huge emotional reaction? He went back to business as usual, and then scripture goes on to start recording the miracles he performed. THAT is what we want for YOU!

Explaining The Mantle

Have you ever heard the saying, "He carried the mantle of leadership well?" So often we've wondered what the heck is the mantle? A mantle we discovered is nothing more than something that covers or surrounds something else. The keywords are surrounds and covers.

Picture a mantle that goes around the fireplace. It covers the fireplace, but then also the fireplace holds it up. We are the ones that hold this mantle. When decorating, isn't it fun to dress up a mantle? A rule of thumb is, it can't be too busy or it takes the emphasis away from the fireplace. If too much is placed on a mantle and weighs it down, then the heaviness is noticed, and the focus is lost.

When this focus is lost we lose balance, and we let the weight of things we're carrying consume the fire that's supposed to be inside us. But if the mantle is too heavy it will smother the fire and put it out. As a lead pastor's wife, we have to "mind the mantle" so to speak in order to protect ourselves from burnout and isolation. If the fire within us is smothered and extinguished then we are not serving our correct purpose. We are not living the full, rich, satisfying destiny God has for each of us.

The mantle is supposed to complement the fireplace, but it can consume us if there is too much stuff on it. If we are consumed with the weight of what is happening it will distort our focus from the true reason why we are in this position. A mantle symbolizes the anointing, spiritual authority, and greater works. It isn't an accident God chose you to wear it. He believes in you.

FROM ROBIN:

I had been a college and career pastor, a worship and arts pastor, an associate pastor, and an evangelist. Jerry and I had worked in many different areas throughout the years. I thought I was well conditioned and aware of what the mantle of senior pastor's wife would feel and look like. After about two years into taking over the church, I asked myself this question, "Why is the weight of this mantle different from what I had experienced in the past?"

I realized the answer to this question was, we now carried the weight of the entire church on our shoulders.

For example, I used to walk into church and think, "Are all the singers here? Are all the musicians ready? Did everyone learn the songs?" and now I walk in and think, "Why are there fingerprints on the front door? Who was supposed to vacuum the lobby? Is the worship team ready to go? Did my husband get enough sleep to preach well? Are the nursery workers here? Are the greeters in place?" While at the same time wondering, "Did that post I read yesterday on Facebook really mean what I think it meant about this church? Is Kelly ever coming back to church because she hasn't been here in three weeks? Will the family who left offended last week, be back this week? Did I thank Sally for the recipe she gave me? Did I ask Bob about his job interview?" and I'm sure you could add your own thoughts to this list.

So at the end of the day, the totality of the job is on your mind, and it turns into a weight you are not fully prepared for until the mantle is yours. Before, I was over a section of the sheep; now I'm over all of them. Even though my husband is the lead pastor, it's a weight we both carry if I am involved in people's lives and care about their discipleship.

We may not have asked for this mantle or ever saw ourselves as a pastor's wife. This mantle may have been thrust upon us. Or you may be like some pastors' wives we have met that grew up always knowing they were going to marry a pastor. Either way, this mantle of leadership was acquired, and it is a privilege to wear. Losing sight of this privilege is where many of us start the trek to our island. We start to resent this position we are in because we are trying to carry too much. We are working in our own strength instead of in God's tender loving care.

We cannot run from this mantle, just like a fireplace cannot jump out of the wall and leave your house. It is ours to wear. If we run away to an unhealthy place, all we do is carry that stinky, nasty, overcrowded, ugly mantle with us. On the other hand, if we dig in, turn around, and look fully at the mantle we are carrying, then we can start to remove what is weighing us down.

Don't be afraid to say no to invitations to baby showers, graduations, parties, and dinners. Even if it is temporary, take some time to figure this out. Let's clean up our mantle and wear it well.

FROM SHEILA:

One of the first times I realized I was allowing others' actions to extinguish the fire inside was when a couple we were great friends with came to our church, and my husband trusted them and put them on staff. This couple ended up lying to us, betraying us, going behind our backs and saying some pretty horrible things about our ministry and us. It was extremely hurtful. They quit and were gone

the next day. I felt like I had been punched in the stomach and slapped across the face.

I started the usual work of trying to forgive, trying not to think about them, and trying not to go through all the conversations I wanted to have, telling them what I thought of their lies and wicked behavior! One night, weeks later, we went to a friend's church for a special meeting, and there they were. I had a hard time concentrating on the message because I was so caught up in my anger toward these people and all they did to my husband and our church.

At the end of the service, I was so convicted that I answered the altar call to repent of my poor behavior. God spoke to me and told me to go pray for the wife of this couple. I wish I could tell you I jumped up and went. Instead, I argued with God and tried to remind Him of how horrible their actions were. God said again to go pray for her, but this time He added, "If you do not obey Me, I will harden your heart."

Those words shook me to the core and scared me half to death. I immediately turned to go find her at her seat, but surprisingly she was standing right behind me! I grabbed her and told her God wanted me to pray for her. She began to weep huge tears as I prayed for her and her family. I could feel the weeks of tension, anger, unforgiveness, and betrayal, melt from me. That prayer, I believe, was much more about my obedience and humbling myself to obey God than about anything else. I had to swallow my pride and do the hard thing, and I am so glad I did. I had started to close myself off from her and anyone like her. I had started to resent the position we were in. I didn't want to go through other hurts such as this one. My inner dialogue consisted of thoughts of not ever hiring friends again or never allowing myself to tell anything personal to people in the church. That was a sure sign of sailing away to the island. I had a responsibility to take the high road and make the first move.

We can't mind the mantle with unforgiveness in our hearts. We become bitter, hard-hearted people when we harbor any unforgiveness, and we tend to isolate ourselves to protect our hearts from further hurt.

Doing The Hard Thing

One of our pastors says H.A.R.D. stands for Hear…Ask…Receive…Do. Hearing God is usually easy. Asking Him for instructions is even doable. Receiving those instructions is a no-brainer. Doing what you've heard, asked for, and received, is another matter entirely. Sometimes He asks us to do things that are easy, that prop us up and make us look really good. We like those days!

There are those other days in which God is asking you to do a hard thing. Those hard moments are usually the exact thing we need to bring growth and blessing into our lives. If God is sending you in a direction you do not want to go, the greatest advice we can give you is to do just that. Go. Grace will cover you. A timely quote from a great book titled, *When Words Hurt*...by Warren Bullock:

"Grace empowers us to transform for our own benefit that which was intended to harm us. Grace harnesses the unconquerable forces of loving, blessing, praying, and doing well. Grace raises a stout defense while affirming the offender. Grace rests in the assurance of God's vindication. Grace develops the character that withstands verbal assault. How do we cope with criticism? How do we deal with the inevitable-hurtful arrows shot at us? How do we keep criticism from derailing our leadership? GRACE! We've received grace from God and now we give grace away to our critics."

Anytime God has asked us to do those hard things and we have done them, later we are always so thankful. If this job were easy everyone would do it right? Taking on this mantle is not for the weak or faint of heart. It's a huge job; it's a hard thing. But the benefits are worth it as we see lives transform and build God's Kingdom.

Your Assignment Should You Choose to Accept It

Write down one thing God is asking you to do that you do not want to do. Look at that thing with no selfish objective. In other words, remove yourself entirely from the equation. Is this a task that someone wearing your mantle can achieve? Is this a task that will bring reconciliation to a relationship? Is this a task that will bring honor and glory to God? Ask yourself those tough questions, answer them, then move on to the action whatever that action may be. Keep in mind the entire time the mantle you wear. You can and must walk a higher road, being an example for others to follow. The outcome isn't always what we romance in our minds. In fact, the hard things we go through may make matters worse for a time. But if God is in it, He will bring good from it. Trust that fact.

ANSWER & APPLY

1. Am I taking on things that aren't mine to carry?

2. Am I good at delegating responsibility or does it feel like I'm losing control when I hand over duties to others?

3. What is one thing I can think of right now that I do not need to be doing, that will help me clear my mantle?

TAKEAWAY

All of the smaller mantles you have carried throughout the years were preparing you for the weight of the big mantle worn now. Don't begrudge the smaller assignments because God is working in and through those to prepare you for greater things. Even though your mantle may seem overwhelming at times God knew you could handle it. He was preparing in advance. If you have moments when you feel very defeated and the weight is just too heavy, you're not alone. It's okay to have those moments of being tired. God never said the weight would be light; He said He would help us carry it.

"The road from your office to mine is 100 miles."
Spoken by a lead pastor to his associate.

Chapter Seven
Reframing Expectations

When he finally came to his senses, he said to himself,
'At home, even the hired servants have food enough to
spare, and here I am dying of hunger!'

Luke 15:17

Why in the world would we include a scripture about the prodigal son in a chapter about unrealistic expectations? Well, we believe this son is the perfect example of the cold hand of reality punching a person in the gut.

When we set out to be a pastor/pastor's wife, we had expectations, dreams, and visions of what life was going to be like. We may have thought life was about to get much easier, or the blessings of God were going to flow like fine wine, or (insert your expectation here). Just like the prodigal, he set out with tons of money and visions of wine, women, and song. Except when that punch hit him he realized…uh…this was not really what I signed up for. Check, please! I'm outta here.

He ended up in the pigsty, realizing what he left. So many times, we end up in the pig pen, too. Except ours looks like a secluded island of walls, with moats surrounding it full of fire breathing dragons placed strategically to keep people out!

Our own unrealistic expectations can send us to this island, and before we know it we long to go home. We want to go back where it's comfortable. Where we had all the amenities. Where we didn't know how mean some people could be, just like the prodigal didn't realize how mean and cruel life could be.

We can easily become disillusioned in ministry by thinking of what our expectations were, compared to the reality around us. When we do not take our thoughts captive we can become very discouraged. These discouraging times come when we start thinking of the past and longing for it, instead of forging ahead to the future God has planned.

JESUS

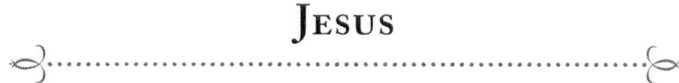

Honestly, why would we think we deserve better treatment than Jesus? He was treated horribly. I can venture to guess none of us have been treated as horribly as He was. We haven't suffered a cruel and humiliating death! Aren't we thankful He didn't go off to an island to avoid the hurt and the pain? Just like people in your life need you, they need your love and wisdom, and your church is going to be glad you came off your island.

Have you ever wondered if Jesus knew what He was going to have to endure from an early age? Do you think He had expectations about His life and ministry that were unrealistic? He was human after all. But the beauty of Jesus is that He loved us enough to move forward even though He knew what lay ahead for Him.

There are people in your life who need you to do the same. Your situation may not change, but that doesn't mean there aren't incredible moments waiting for you.

OTHERS' UNREALISTIC EXPECTATIONS

Sometimes it can be frustrating when others have expectations of us that we try to meet and can't. We will run around crazy if we try to meet everyone else's expectations. What one person may expect, another person may think is shameful. Our best advice is…you be you. The very best version of YOU! Because there is never going to be a time we will meet everyone's expectations of who they think we should be. We have an audience of One to make happy and that's what we have to stay focused on.

From Sheila:

I have two stories to tell you of others' expectations on us. The first one came when our church moved away from the theater and got into a building where everything was new to us.

Jack and I were excited so we showed up the first few Sundays really early at the same time the worship team was arriving. After a couple of Sundays doing this, a woman remarked, "Do you guys not trust us to do everything right? Is that why you guys are always here so early?"

Of course, that was not the reason at all, and nothing could have been further from our minds. Compare that remark to several months later as we started arriving at 8:00 am, still, a full hour before anything began, but later than we had arrived before. We were on our way and got a call from a distraught wife in our church saying her husband, who was trying to beat a drug addiction, was threatening suicide. We took a detour immediately to their home and arrived before the police. We stayed with them and talked him down, and when the police arrived they took over. We were sad and upset but made our way to church and still arrived at 8:45 am.

As soon as I walked through the door a man looked at his watch and said, "I wish I was allowed to lay in bed on Sunday mornings and arrive whenever I wanted." If I could put emoji's in this book I would place the little one here that has its mouth hanging open and hands on each

cheek. These were unrealistic expectations others were placing on us to make us feel guilty or bad for not doing what they expected. What I had to realize is that they had no idea what was going on in our reasons or actions. Now, when someone says insane remarks like these I just go with them. I agree, I usually restate the remark back to them like, "Yeah I ran out of bonbons. That's the only reason I got out of bed this morning." And I keep walking. It backs them off and makes them laugh, and most times they realize their remark is stupid.

Another area that makes our efforts impossible to fulfill others' expectations is the ministry gifts. There are different gifts given to different pastors, as God allows. If we all were the same personality or had the same gift, we could not make up a healthy body (the Church).

When a pastor and his wife take over an already established church, there may be a lot of unwritten rules about what to do and what not to do. There may also be a lot of comparing the new guy to the old guy.

FROM ROBIN:

Jerry is more of an apostle type leader. The pastor who had this church before us was great but different than Jerry. There were many at the church who wanted Jerry to act just like the pastor before us, and it was impossible. He didn't naturally do the things the previous pastor did. He had other gifts and talents that were for this body of believers. Many got offended because he was not being who they wanted him to be. He was not fulfilling their expectations. It was no fault of his, they were just unwilling to be flexible, opening, and show grace to their new leader.

Apostles are generally focused toward more kingdom-minded thinking. So, when Jerry walks by ten people and doesn't stop and talk to every one of them, people may take that as unfriendliness. Nothing could be further from the truth. His actions are driven and purposeful, not that talking to everyone is without purpose, but when something is on his mind for the kingdom there is no stopping him.

When Jerry and I took the church, there were a list of rules that were unacceptable that were completely unattainable. We came in and told everyone we were not that guy. We celebrated the guy before us but made sure everyone knew this was a new era for the church.

One night, though, we saw what others' expectations of us can drive them toward. It was a cold winter night, and my husband and I had to be at the church for prayer. A couple called and wanted to meet with us and basically get off their chest all that didn't satisfy them about me, Jerry, and the church. I promise you one of the things they brought up was this…they were not getting the church emails in their alerts. Instead, they were going into their junk file. My first thought was this, and it's not very pastor like. AND??…SERIOUSLY??? Why is this our problem??? We are in a culture where people have no idea what they want; they just think we can do it all.

We enter ministry with all these expectations that our communities are going to be set on fire. We will have hundreds or even thousands coming to our church in no time. Then after many years, we may still only have 100 people, and our expectations are not met.

It's easy to become discouraged and defeated when what we saw in our minds does not pan out to be realistic. Many times, in this situation we lose our focus because now we think we have failed.

Reframe Focus

In reality, what we need to do is reframe our focus. Doing this doesn't mean we are settling for less than what God has called us to. It means we are allowing ourselves to see the victory in what has happened. Mark 5:11-12 is a great example of this very thing. When people treat us badly, we have to remember we are racking up treasure in heaven!

When we reframe our focus, it is at this point we give ourselves permission to stop with the pity party. Instead of asking all the "why" questions, we can say, "Hey, you know what? Things may not be happening like I thought they would or like I want, but I'm going to choose to be successful today!" Then decide to press in, do more, give of yourself again, don't back down, and never give up.

Look for victories in the small things.

FROM SHEILA:

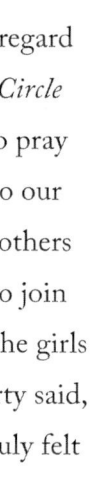

I was at a very discouraging place a few years ago in regard to our church. I had just read Mark Batterson's *The Circle Maker*. He got me pumped up and so I wanted to go pray circles around the property that had been donated to our church. I needed to do something productive. I told others on our church's Facebook page so whoever wanted to join me could. Only about ten people showed up. One of the girls who came and prayed as we walked across that property said, "Where is everybody? This is disappointing." But I truly felt encouraged by those ten people. Instead of focusing on who wasn't there, I became very grateful for who WAS there. It wasn't discouraging to me at all. My encouragement came because I had chosen to reframe my focus. Before I read that book I more than likely would have felt the same way my friend did because of the low turnout.

Of course, my friend Robin knew of my discouragement during that time, and when I got back in my car

she called. She had been praying for me and felt
God tell her to tell me, "We cannot let what happens for
three hours on Sunday mornings define our entire ministry,
and that for every couple who had left our church,
He would replace them with two." :)

This word is actually taken straight from Isaiah 61:7-8. I was
very grateful for her encouragement. We cannot let Sunday
mornings define our entire lives in ministry. As pastors and
pastors' wives, we have victories all week long through
phone calls, crisis moments, encouraging someone
through a text or visit, and hospital visits.

We cannot worry or continue to try to fulfill everyone else's expectations of us. Allow God to show you how these people who are in your church are His. Not yours. When we pour into their lives, that is us stewarding His son or daughter well. It is our honor to show Jesus to the person who is in front of us. If they leave us tomorrow we will know we did what God asked. If we get hurt and then carry that hurt around, we're taking ownership of something we have no business owning. Those are hurts that were never meant for us to carry. It's our choice.

Reframe your focus to be able to see reality differently. And do not hesitate to celebrate who God made you. If He wanted you to be the pastor's wife who was there before you, He would have made you her!

Answer & Apply

1. Do I buy into the bad press others want to publish about me?

2. Am I a people-pleaser? If so, Explain.

3. What is one problem I have right now? Write it down and then list three things that you are grateful for surrounding that problem.

Takeaway

People have expectations that they themselves can't even achieve. We used to let this bother us, and maybe some days it still does, but we've learned to brush it off and do our best. Robin's father said this years ago… "Jesus was perfect, and they still found fault. They still hung Him on a cross." Those words of wisdom set Robin free, and we hope they have the same effect on you. We are not God; we are not superman. We are just good old human beings with a supernatural God to guide us. Don't let others' expectations trip you up.

"The prodigal son lost everything before he realized what he had. He reframed his expectations and recognized he had a good life all along at the place he originally didn't want to be. We have to allow ourselves to celebrate the s mall wins, being grateful for every step along the way."

~ Sheila Harper ~

Chapter Eight

Sowing Love And Honor

And because of their unbelief, He couldn't do any miracles

among them except to place His hands on a few

sick people and heal them.

Mark 6:5

If you have been in ministry any time at all, you have probably seen your husband be dishonored. His birthday comes and goes with nothing more than a "Happy Birthday" from a few church members. Pastor Appreciation Month comes and goes year after year with nothing more than a pat on the back. Many times, not even these things I mentioned may have happened.

I'm sure there are other scenarios you are thinking of right now, the confrontations, the wicked words spoken, and the hateful emails. Hopefully you have a great congregation who loves to honor their pastor and his wife, but unfortunately, there are times that is not the case.

When we take a look at Mark 6:5 through the eyes of honor, we have to see that Jesus was held back from doing what He does best because of a lack of honor. When you read the whole chapter, you understand He was dealing with people who knew Him well. They were looking at Him as Mary's son or that carpenter's kid. There was a spirit of familiarity. They let this familiar spirit cloud their vision of who He really was. Because of their shortsightedness, He was unable to heal all the people who were sick.

Contrast this scenario with other scenarios of Jesus healing everyone He came in contact with in other cities. They believed He was who He said He was, therefore showing Him honor.

THERE'S A REWARD FOR HONOR

"A lack of honor can cut off our reward," says John Bevere in his book, *Honor's Reward*. The people who honored Jesus got what they needed. The people who didn't honor Jesus received nothing.

We don't want this to happen to you. We made the correlation here, and we want you to as well. When we're living on an island, we're not trusting Jesus to take care of us. We're not honoring Him after He called us to the position we're in. We may have convinced everyone in the church we are just fine, but in our hearts, we are guarded and have them locked tighter than Fort Knox.

Matthew15:8 says, "These people honor me with their lips, but their hearts are far from Me." Could Jesus be talking about you? I know at one time He could have been talking about us. We put on our church smiles and marched to church determining in our hearts no one was ever going to get close to us again.

Ladies, this is not the way to honor the God who has given you life and a privileged mantle to wear. There is a better way!

GET REAL

When we put on our church smiles and talk to everyone knowing in our hearts we are guarded and distant, we are restraining the works of Jesus in our own lives. We're saying, "I don't trust you to watch out for me, so I'm going to take care of myself."

We are not advocating you go tell everyone everything, but we are encouraging you to be more real and open with people. Let them see the you that is vulnerable, the you that is not made up all the time, the you that hurts and cries on occasion, the you that likes a good football game. Are we making sense?

Make your heart line up with your mouth. Don't allow two different scenarios to be going on in there. Have a good talk with your heart now and then and ask what is troubling it. Be honest, you may fool the church people, but you will never fool God.

I love how the Message Bible states 2 John 1:8, "And be very careful around them so you don't lose out on what we've worked so diligently in together; I want you to get every reward you have coming to you."

Here are a couple of examples of honor and how we believe giving honor has brought incredible reward into these precious lives.

From Sheila:

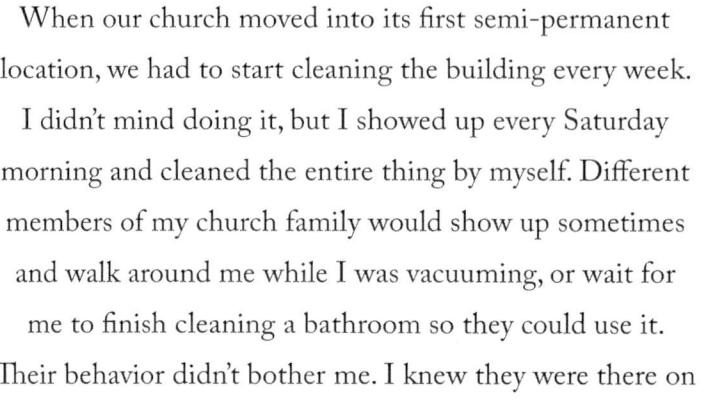

When our church moved into its first semi-permanent location, we had to start cleaning the building every week. I didn't mind doing it, but I showed up every Saturday morning and cleaned the entire thing by myself. Different members of my church family would show up sometimes and walk around me while I was vacuuming, or wait for me to finish cleaning a bathroom so they could use it. Their behavior didn't bother me. I knew they were there on a Saturday morning for a different reason, and that was fine. I cleaned every Saturday for about six months until a couple from our church, Harold, and Mary, had to come by one Saturday morning.

They saw that I was cleaning and went right into action. Their words, "No pastor's wife of ours is going to be cleaning this building!" They then took over the cleaning duties and accomplished this task each week, or found someone else for the next two years until we got into our permanent location. They never complained. They didn't get offended if they weren't recognized for their service in public, nor did they tell others they were cleaning. They just cleaned. They found this service a privilege to do for God's house and for me. I could not have felt more honored than they made me feel. Where are they today you ask? Mary is now the director of women's ministries at our church, and Harold has been repeatedly promoted and now is the prison chaplain for one of our state prison locations. He also serves on our church board. Sowing honor comes with a reward.

These people are the real deal. They "get" the value of honor, and their reward has shown up repeatedly in their lives and their family's lives because of the generous honor they have sown.

FROM ROBIN:

One time we had MRSA strike one of the kids at our church. We didn't find out until Saturday afternoon. Word spread quickly, and several of the moms completely freaked out. I know it was for good reason, but instead of helping fix the problem, they inundated me with texts and phone calls telling me all the things "we" should do…close down the nursery, hire a professional to come and clean, call all the families in the church who could have been exposed…etc. etc. These were all good ideas, but not one person offered to help me do all these things. By now it was 9:00 pm before we could assess the situation fully. I went to the church by myself and started one by one the arduous task of cleaning/bleaching every toy and every item in our nursery.

A girl from our church, Amy, and her daughter found out what was going on and came straight to the church working alongside me until midnight. I felt very honored that Amy would not let me do that all by myself. Amy showed great honor to me by inconveniencing herself and spending her Saturday night scrubbing down the nursery when she could have been in bed, and with her family. Today Amy and I are still great friends and I cherish every moment we get to spend together.

These are two great examples of what it is like to "sow" honor into another's life. We included these stories because we have to follow their example. Harold, Mary, Amy, and her daughter did not spend all that time because they knew, in the end, they would get promoted. That was just what naturally happened in God's system of doing things. There is a great reward when we love and honor selflessly.

This is what awaits us as we sow love and honor into other people's lives that God has given us to shepherd. You may not have such a story of your church members wanting to honor you by taking care of you. In fact, this may seem foreign. But people will follow your example. As you lead by sowing honor and love into others not only will you reap these things in your own life, but they will, in turn, learn from your example. You will change the culture of your church by making sure love and honor are distinguished and constant guests in your attitude and actions.

AGATHOPOIEO

As a pastor's wife, you may have had someone tell a lie about you, maybe even multiple lies. These actions could have played a part in why you may have ended up on the island in the first place.

We have talked about the reasons we shouldn't be on the island earlier in this book, but let's look a little bit deeper. When we seclude ourselves, we leave our perceptions of who we are, up to others' imaginings. We keep people from seeing the real, authentic person we are. Therefore, if an accusation is made no one knows if it's true or not. They do not know us, so they can only wonder. BUT! I have good news for you. There is a verse found in 1 Peter 2:15 that says,

"It is God's will that your honorable lives should silence those ignorant people who make foolish accusations against you."

How cool is that scripture? Honorable in the Greek is the word "agathopoieo". Don't ask us how to say it because we don't know! But we can tell you the definition, which is, "to do something which profits others, be a good help to someone".

So, what this passage is telling us is that when we do things that profit others, (love and honor) then our lives will speak for themselves. If people know the authentic us, then our past behavior of sowing love and honor will shut down the critics. When the lie gets passed from person to person it will hit the ears of the ones who have seen your honorable life. They will, in turn, realize who the betrayer is, and more than likely the lie will die a quick death.

This incredible outcome does not happen if we are living on an island by ourselves. We must come off the island, live an honorable life, and the results will take care of themselves!

ANSWER & APPLY

1. What does honor mean to me?

2. How do I practice honor?

3. Do I withhold love when others withhold honor?

4. What can I do to "up my game" when it comes to honor?

TAKEAWAY

This book… *The Culture of Honor* by Danny Silk is an amazing book. We highly recommend it to you and your staff if you've not read it. It will change your life. The basic theme behind this book is; if you want to thrive and please God your foundation has to include honoring one another. There is no better takeaway we can give you with this chapter than to point you toward this remarkable resource.

"True honor is an outflow from a heart that fears God."

~ John Bevere ~

CHAPTER NINE
THINKING LONG

But those who trust in the Lord will find new strength.
They will soar high on wings like eagles. They will run and
not grow weary. They will walk and not faint.

ISAIAH 40:31

Wait patiently for the Lord. Be brave and courageous.
Yes, wait patiently for the Lord.

PSALM 27:14

Yes, we have two scriptures for you in this chapter because we want you to get familiar with both. They are profound truths, if heeded, will benefit us all in the long run.

The key words in these passages are:

- trust

- find strength

- soar high

- run

- not grow weary

- wait patiently

- be brave

- courageous

- wait patiently (2 x's)

Usually, if God says something twice in a row it's because this is a concept He wants us to pay particularly close attention to. Waiting patiently is usually not our strong suit is it, Ladies? But wait patiently, we must. *(said in Yoda voice)*

WAITING PATIENTLY AND ALL THAT STUFF

The concept of "thinking long" came from a book written by Mark Batterson called, *The Circle Maker*. It is an incredible book we have both read and gained much insight from. We hope all of you will read it, too.

In the book, he discusses at length the concept of thinking long. We live in a society where everything is in a flash. We punch a button on a computer, and in lightning speed, our words go to outer space and back in less than a second. We have grown accustomed to having everything NOW.

So, when we see this guy or that guy go and start a church with three people, and six months later they're running 30,000, we think, "Well, he made that look easy. I'm sure we can do that too!" We just assume that is the norm because that is who and what got press time. We skip right over all the churches within a twenty-mile radius of us that have less than 200 people in them. Instead, we look to the guy who is the absolute exception to the norm, and we compare ourselves to him.

You may look at your own situation and see that you are ten years into this church plant, and you still only have 100 people. Compared to the "started with three people" guy we look like a complete failure in our own eyes. This type of thinking could drive us to the island and make a cynic out of us. We cannot allow the thoughts of *nothing has changed, nothing is ever going to change* to occupy our minds.

Just because our churches may not have grown to meet our expectations, it doesn't mean we stop waiting patiently or thinking long. We must maintain a mindset of long-term thinking. Just because things haven't happened according to our timeline doesn't mean they are never going to happen.

We have to stop allowing the comparison trap to snag us. Comparison can cause us to hurry and doubt God's timeline. And if we doubt God's timeline we may miss the very thing we hoped for. God's timing is very rarely, if ever, our timing.

God's Timeline

Have you ever noticed that God's timeline is always different from our own? If you're like me, it seems God's answer is never going to show up when I think I need it, but it always does at the precise time I truly need it. Just ask Abraham and Sarah if it's ever too late to see a promise come true. They had absolutely no hope of ever having a child, and God made a way. God was "thinking long" for them.

FROM SHEILA:

We planted the church in November of 2007. In June of 2010, after meeting each week in a local movie theater, we had a man call and say he was going to donate a nearly nine-acre piece of land to us. This was through a series of total God-events that I would love to sit down and tell you some day. We thought we would certainly have the deed the next week. Month after month went by. Several men in the church started to look at my husband with suspicion thinking he had been duped.

My husband had read Deuteronomy 11:24, and he started having regular prayer times on the land where the church would walk all around, over, and through that property claiming it would truly be ours someday. For one reason or another, it took months to complete paperwork, surveys, and appraisals. Finally, Christmas of that same year we received the deed. It was a true miracle, but now we needed to build.

Our prayers changed at that point, and we began to picture and believe in faith that God would provide a way for us to build on that land and have a permanent church meeting place. We continued to walk that property. We had all night prayer meetings on that parcel of land. We mowed it, cleaned it, and believed for a building all together, and finally, FIVE YEARS LATER we broke ground.

Five years may not seem like a long time, but when you're in the middle of waiting and being questioned on a constant basis it is a VERY long time. I will forever be grateful for my husband's ability to think long. He never gave up hope that we would have a structure on that land. We now have three structures on that land, and they are absolutely beautiful to all of us. We thought long as a church family, and several who were short-term thinkers couldn't make the transition with us. The pioneers, the walking-on-water-faith-believers, are now reaping the benefits of their incredible sticktoitiveness. Did I think it would take five years? No. But now all of that is in the past, and we now have a launching pad for greater ministry than we ever dreamed.

What trips us up when it comes to timelines is thinking short term. We go into a new city and take over a church, or plant a church, and we imagine it blowing up with growth! We imagine all we're going to do for God and how the city is going to be transformed. That's all great, but in reality, our timelines rarely happen like we think. When we do this, we almost set ourselves up to fail.

We may have come from a big city or a mega church, and we have all this information to bring to the table. We think God has equipped us with all this experience, and what we find is that people don't really care about our experience and talent. They don't care about our information, and sometimes we find people may even resent all our "talent". Many pastor's wives are devastated when circumstances do not play out like they thought. You assume if God sent you there, everyone is going to love you, you're going to make a huge difference, and the church is going to grow! Oftentimes, that is not the case.

From Robin:

When Jerry and I moved to Jasper, we had so many dreams, visions, and promises that we just knew the whole town was going to explode! We were bringing so much of all we did musically to Jasper and we had no doubt we would take the city by storm. What we experienced could not have been further from our dreams.

People didn't want to hear about how we did things in Atlanta that were mega-successful. They didn't care about the thousands of people we had ministered

to through drama. We slowly realized we were in a small town, and their thinking is very different from fast-paced Atlanta.

A few years into taking over this church, we weren't growing. In fact, people had left us after saying they were excited we were there. Our children were moving away, and it was a very tough time for us.

I came home one night, sat down with my little doggy Buttons and sobbed my eyes out. I truly felt like Buttons was my only friend in the whole world. I felt like Dorothy just wanting to find my way back to Kansas. My entire identity as a person had been yanked out from under me. Everything I loved had been taken away, and I had no hope for the future. I didn't feel like I belonged or fit in anywhere. I was a mess.

Couple that with the fact the city had told us they were going to build a road right beside our church that connected to the freeway, but years later…no road. We knew that road would bring hundreds maybe even thousands more to our church. As of right now, we are hidden in a neighborhood.

After this long cry session with Buttons, I raised myself up and decided to obliterate discouragement in my life. I started reminding myself of all that HAD gone right. People's lives WERE being transformed, people were meeting

Jesus, and we were being used by God to touch this small town. I began to be grateful for these things, and my mood quickly changed.

We focused on our commitment and had to work purposefully to not allow discouragement in. We refused to give in or give up on what God had called us to do. Now, fast forward years later, and we are so grateful God helped us "think long". Not only is the road being built and crews are working every day, but I have some of the most loyal women surrounding me that I have ever had in my life. Thinking long pays off. Making the devil flee from your thoughts makes the thinking long process easier! If we had left this town we would have never experienced these realizations. The value of our property and the visibility of our church has increased dramatically.

Thinking long became a reality to Robin. Just because we have been told something, doesn't mean it's going to happen that second, that day, or even that year. Thinking long keeps our focus on future promises, future hope, and most importantly on the Lord who is the only One who can bring these promises to pass.

Answer & Apply

1. Do I feel like I live in a constant state of impatience?

2. Do I take the time to celebrate baby steps?

3. What does succeeding in this area look like to me?

4. Does this success have a timeframe? If so, explain.

Takeaway

Our hope is based on God and not our circumstances. He has reminded us time and time again that He is our help in any present time of challenge. We've had times in our ministry where we felt hopeless, and it was in those very times God reminded us He was in control, and the enemy is a liar. It's common in ministry to let the things that are going on really drain our peace, but at the end of the day God is our peace and hope!!! He is working all of it for our good. He has a plan that may not have been revealed to us just yet. THINK LONG ANYWAY!

"Prayer doesn't just change circumstances. More importantly, it changes us. It doesn't just alter external realities. It alters internal realities so that we see with spiritual eyes. It gives us peripheral vision. It corrects our nearsightedness. It enables us to see beyond our circumstances, beyond ourselves, beyond time."

Mark Batterson from sermon on *"Thinking Long"*

PART THREE:

LIVING OFF THE ISLAND

How do you think Mary felt when an angel of the Lord appeared and told her she would be pregnant with the Son of God? Have you ever pondered the fear she must have faced and the ridicule she probably endured? I'm sure every day was a struggle for her. Do you ever wonder why God picked her?

What an incredible honor to be chosen by God to carry His Son. During this process, she was put on display among shepherds and wise men, hunted by an evil king named Herod and gave birth in a barn to the Savior of the world. She had no choice but to accept her calling and press in. Her life and the baby she carried would change the course of history. Was it worth it? I would proclaim a resounding YES!!!

Everything Mary went through had a purpose and was designed to carry out God's plan for mankind. We still participate in His story today. We have to trust God and believe that He is working all these things for our good. If Mary had hidden away and never accepted her mission where would we be today? Someone out there will be changed by your perseverance. Someone will know the Lord as their personal Savior all because you didn't give up. Take those steps of faith, Ladies. Imagine your feet taking those vital steps back to the reason they were created. It's a lot less lonely on the mainland.

CHAPTER TEN
I HAVE A FIRST NAME TOO

"For we are God's masterpiece. he has created us
anew in Christ Jesus, so we can do the good things
He planned for us long ago."

EPHESIANS 2:10

If we had to guess, there are days when the only introduction you get is, "Meet Pastor Tom's wife" or "This is the preacher's wife" or "Have you met my pastor's wife?" We know often times this is a sign or recognition of honor, and we appreciate that. But when you have a personal relationship with a person and instead of saying, "Meet my friend, Robin" or "I want to introduce you to my friend, Sheila" they don't use your first name, it's just a little odd to us.

In what other profession do we do that to a person, introducing a woman only as a husband's profession? After a while, this could take a toll on an individual. If you feel as though your plans, your dreams, your individuality is being quashed, then it becomes easy to sail away to the island. Also, this works in the other direction as well. When your church family repeats this introduction multiple times they start to believe that's who you are, too. You feel completely defined by your husband's job, driving home the feeling of losing who you truly are and being swallowed up by "pastor's wifedom."

Don't believe your own press. You may feel the weight of unspoken expectations being introduced this way. You may try incredibly hard to meet those elusive expectations of what everyone else thinks you should be. But ultimately who you are, is not your position or role. It's the person who God is making you to be! If you start to think of yourself as a role to play, then you will find yourself performing and overanalyzing relationships, making you less willing to engage with other women as the real person you are.

FROM ROBIN:

I've been Steven's mom, Matthew's mom, Lauren's mom, and Jerry's wife. Wearing every one of those titles is a privilege and precious to me. But sometimes I just don't want

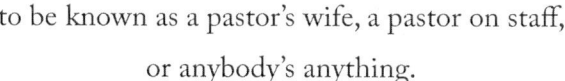

to be known as a pastor's wife, a pastor on staff, or anybody's anything.

Sometimes I want to let my hair down and just be known as Robin. If I'm going through pain I don't want to have to act like I'm okay when I'm not, and I want the right to do that.

Often times people will assume you are a certain way because of your title, and that's just frustrating. We may not be like that at all, but people will automatically assume we're judgmental, or stuck up, or whatever label they have placed on the title of pastor's wife. I never introduce myself as "I'm the pastor's wife at New Beginnings". I say, "I'm Robin."

There's also an expectation of what we're supposed to be that is unrealistic at times. Just recently I had a conversation with a retired pastor's wife, and she told me of how her pastor's wife didn't show up at a function. The church people were hurt because she didn't show up. I asked her why that was expected of the pastor's wife. Why is she required or expected to be at every single thing the church does? She didn't really give me an answer, I think most do not realize they place these unrealistic expectations on us. Unrealistic expectations are enough to drive someone crazy. I'm just Robin. I like to play jokes on people, and it has nothing to do with being a pastor's wife. It's who I am.

Let Your Hair Down

Let's get honest, sometimes you just don't want to talk church. For us to maintain a healthy relationship with our churches and church families, there are times we need to just lay ministry down for a little while. Now, that doesn't mean we walk away from who we are, but there are times it's okay to just let your hair down and have girl time, me time, fun time!

We have often thought people do not see pastor's wives as normal girls, with normal emotions, wanting to do normal everyday things. They can't imagine us lying around in our pajamas all day eating chocolate and popcorn and watching Hallmark movies.

For instance, Robin likes reading a good novel, going to the beach, and decorating. Sheila likes hiking, reading, and writing. Okay, that totally just felt like we were trying out for a pageant, but you know what I mean? We just like to be us sometimes, not someone's mom, not someone's wife, not someone's anything, just Sheila…and just Robin.

There's a scene that is SO TRUE from the movie, "Mom's Night Out" with Patricia Heaton. If you haven't seen this movie, you should rent it today. It's hilarious, but anyway, Patricia is a pastor's wife. Some ladies in her church invite her to go out with them, and she looks so shocked like she can't believe someone would want her to go out with them just for fun. That is a very real scene from many a pastor's wife's life. They don't get invitations because everyone thinks they're so busy, or they don't get invitations because everyone thinks she will stifle their fun, or they don't get invitations because everyone thinks they'll have to pray and read their Bible all night. None of the above are true about any pastor's wife we know.

There are times when we talk to people, and we don't want to just talk about the church. We're normal girls who like regular conversation just like other girls.

CREATING YOUR OWN SPACE

Sometimes we have to create an environment where we're forced to talk about things other than church.

FROM SHEILA:

When we first started the church, I wasn't sure what my role would be, so I made it my goal to take care of the pastors' wives on staff and the women pastors on staff. The first place I started was recognizing their birthdays. We would pick a night close to her birthday, and then all of us would show up with inexpensive gifts, funny cards, and we split her dinner. It was an easy way to say we love you and make her feel special. It was also an excellent way of making memories.

As our staff grew it became harder and harder to find a night close to her birthday when we could all be together, so sometimes although a birthday may be in June, we couldn't find a night until October! We dubbed these nights our "unbirthdays." Then it didn't matter if we celebrated close to that special day or night; in fact, it was more fun to get presents, not on our birthdays. It made all of us feel extra special.

As the fun grew, our purpose grew, and we began to notice we all liked international foods. We named ourselves

the "International Food Queens" and then later shortened that to IFQ's. So now when we get together we "call an IFQ meeting". We have eaten at back alley Korean markets, upscale Turkish restaurants, and greasy taco stands. We have laughed until one of us almost pees our pants. We have bonded, told stories, embarrassed each other, had initiations, cried over situations for each other, gotten into deep theological conversations over sushi, (all with our matching scarves) and have offered each other a respite from ministry stress and worries. We have realized over the years we need each other. We need these nights to just go out and have fun without any expectations.

These nights have nourished my soul. These girls have sharpened me far beyond anything they can imagine. Even though the faces change periodically, and we may mourn a loss of someone leaving the staff, we know God is going to bring us, someone, to fill the gap. We've learned to be okay with that.

Anybody who doesn't have an emotional and mental break from ministry will eventually burn out and shut down. We have to have relationships that remind us of who we truly are.

Create an environment to just be a girl. You still have to have some degree of separation, but there are times you can ask to just be treated like another girlfriend. This isn't about ministering to each other; it's all about fun.

We live in a transparent world, and we tell so much more about ourselves than our grandparents did. You have to use wisdom, though. Be transparent enough to get off your island. It's okay to let others know you're hurting, but you don't have to tell all the details. They don't need to know all the other distractions. We're not suggesting that you distrust people, but what we are suggesting is keeping a reverence for the office you hold. Publishing all the dirty details of marital struggles or details about hurts within the church doesn't glorify God.

ANSWER & APPLY

1. Do I feel secure in my identity? If yes-Explain how and why. If no-Explain how and why.

2. Do I carve out time just for me? (bubble bath, read a good novel, etc…) If not, then what is one thing you can do for yourself as a treat this week?

3. Do I feel guilty taking that time for myself?

4. How can taking time for myself benefit my relationship with God? My relationship with my husband/family? My position as a pastor's wife?

TAKEAWAY

We want you to give yourself a free pass day. You need a day you don't have to go out or answer any questions. Take days to unplug and spend time with God. We all need time to meditate on God's word and work through our challenges without feeling pressure. And, be sure to take some days to do the things you love. Eventually, you'll get through this challenging season and realize how much wiser you've grown.

Chapter Eleven

Intimacy

Give honor to marriage, and remain faithful to one
another in marriage. God will surely judge people who
are immoral and those who commit adultery.

Hebrews 13:4

Honor in this verse when in its original language means "as of a great price or precious". Think about what you hold as precious. Your "precious" may be a child, a grandchild, a precious family heirloom, or an expensive diamond ring. What do you do with it? You safeguard it. You put it in a special place in your home or you brag about it to your friends. You post pictures of it on Facebook, or you may sacrifice your own wants or needs to make this "precious" better. This is how we must treat our marriages.

When you have been married a long time, it's easy to just fall into a mundane existence where things just happen. You don't have to really work at it anymore because you're so used to each other you live for your work, or the weekends with your kids, or whatever your favorites are. Before you know it, your marriage has become more like roommates instead of an intimate married couple. This is not what Jesus designed marriage to be.

Is It Stress?

We know this is a delicate subject. It's a subject that has to be addressed. When we are giving of ourselves all the time, life can get sucked right out of us. When we're under constant stress and strain it plays out in our homes.

Certain people from the church may always be complaining things aren't going right. You know how hard your husband is working and that he is a good person, but he may not have the personality to address the issues. When this happens, there is a secret resentment that starts to be harbored. This puts stress on a marriage and sends you off to the island.

If you feel like everything is a mess and you're not seeing progress with things getting fixed, these moments are going to affect a woman differently than a man. As women, we are affected by our surroundings. If our houses are clean we're in a great mood. If something is broken in the house then it seems everything is out of control.

There are times we go to bed emotionally and mentally exhausted. Many pastors have high blood pressure, intestinal issues, and many other stress-related ailments. He is dealing with his own set of issues, and so are you, so intimacy falls incredibly low on the list of priorities.

So many times, as the pastor's wife you're counseling couples about the importance of intimacy, and in your own life intimacy is an issue. Then when we get to a certain age some of us have become uncomfortable with our bodies because they're just not perky like they used to be. We live with so much guilt because of these issues, and again, a lot of this can be attributed to stress.

FROM ROBIN:

In the middle of a very painful time in our ministry, Jerry called about 15 minutes before I was getting off work. He said, "You wanna ride the motorcycle?" I said, "YES!" The weather was perfect for a ride. I pulled in the driveway, and he already had the bike pulled out and my helmet in hand. I literally put my purse down in the garage and climbed on the back of the bike.

We drove 30 minutes up the mountain near our home and had a great dinner. It was early fall but we blasted Michael Buble Christmas music loudly and sang at the top of our lungs all the way up there. We ordered everything we wanted at this little pizza place that had a candle on the table. We talked about life and nothing about ministry. We sang Christmas music all the way home again, and when we got home nothing was standing in the way of intimacy.

We realized it was such a simple date, but it was so needed and just relaxed us. We escaped and didn't go with anybody else. It was just me and him, and we knew if all else fails we have each other forever and always. I thought about that date for weeks; it was so special to me. All of these things make a woman feel treasured. It's huge to have nights where the church is not brought home, and we are simply just a couple or a family.

SEX

Sex for a man is a stress release. Sex for a woman sometimes seems as though it's another person wanting something from her. We want to be intimate, it's not that we don't want to be, but there are all these things that hang in the balance of intimacy.

Sometimes we are so overwhelmed with the responsibilities God has given us that when it comes time for intimacy with our spouses we're completely depleted. When we lose intimacy with our spouse then what have we gained?

When we are going through a difficult season, the stress, the load, and the expectations can shut us down intimately. There are times you may not feel like you have the energy to be intimate. Stress can cause weight. When we are going thru a difficult season, the stress, the load, the expectations it can shut you down intimately. You may not feel like you have the energy to be intimate.

Stress can cause weight gain and crazy things to happen to our skin. It can make us lose sleep and fight depression. If we eat to relieve stress, then it will show on our bodies, and we will be ashamed.

Sex connects us to our husbands like nothing else. God created it for pleasure! But when it comes time for intimacy, we are all bogged down with the stressors of the church, our lives, laundry, phone, dishes, kids, school, and it's very hard for us to relax.

We cannot let the church bleed into every facet of our lives. When there are problems at the church, then we tend to let that affect our personal lives. We bring it into the house and spend more time focusing on the church than honoring our marriages and treating each other as precious by keeping the problems at work. We want to encourage you to make a decision to enjoy your spouse and turn off social media and phones and all the unrest those can bring. Talk about other things besides church stuff and have fun together. Your identity is more than the church.

FROM SHEILA:

Jack and I were headed toward a lack of intimacy in our marriage. We had so many problems with the church when we started that it was what we both talked about and dwelt on constantly. It ate up so much of our thought lives and conversation. During the week, we would tell each other we would turn off our computers and just have some free time at night. I would work toward having those 3-4 hours before bedtime to just rest, have a nice dinner and lead a normal life. Of course, something always happened to fill that time with church or something from my ministry, SaveOne.

A few years into the church plant I started resenting the church because we never rested! We never took a day off. Instead of looking in the mirror at what was causing this to happen, I blamed the church. We were a church plant for goodness sake, and there was so much to be done. How could anyone take a day off? God, in His loving way, showed us both the need for a Sabbath.

We decided together we would start taking Fridays off. We made no apologies for being militant about it. God made this command one of the Top 10 for a reason. I think He wants us to take it seriously. So, Fridays turned into "Free Fridays." We were technology free, phone free, and work free. It was a day for us to just spend together free from the phone ringing, free from social media, and free from work.

I began to post about Free Fridays, and even after doing this for several years I still have people make snide comments. That's just life. I know I'm making God happy. But you know what else has happened? I'm much happier. I feel much more free. My husband and I are back to having deep, intimate conversations. We are having fun with each other on Fridays as we scope out new coffeehouses or hike with our hammocks in tow and then hang for a while. I have stopped resenting the church and how much we work because I know Friday is coming, and we can rest. It has been one of the best decisions we have ever made. Free Fridays brought back intimacy and an enjoyment of life again. God knew what we needed. Sabbath rest is not an option.

ANSWER & APPLY

1. When was the last time I went on a date with my husband, like a real date with no other couples or kids?

2. When was the last time I turned my phone off for an extended period of time?

3. When was the last time I had a meaningful conversation with my husband?

4. Plan a date night. Make it happen. Do whatever it takes, and then continue to make it happen at least once per month, preferably more often. Make time to just have fun with your spouse.

TAKEAWAY

If the enemy can rob you of intimate time with your soulmate he can begin the breakdown of your relationship. Go on dates, take walks in the park, or rent a movie from Redbox and cuddle. Your husband is the second most important relationship you have.

CHAPTER TWELVE

CABINET KEEPERS

Most of all love each other as if your life depended on
it. Love makes up for practically anything.

1 PETER 4:8 MSG

There is an old show that used to be on television called "West Wing." It showed the ins and outs of politics and all that would go on in the White House on a day-to-day basis. There is one phrase that sticks out from that show that was repeated often. I believe this phrase would be good for us if we allowed ourselves to think like this. If one of the president's cabinet members was asked to do something good or bad their answer was always, "I serve at the pleasure of the president." In other words, no matter what he asked them to do they did it. Period. No questions asked. They had his back. They kept him well.

The president's cabinet serves a man. We are serving GOD! How much more important is our YES? Do we serve at His pleasure? Or do we argue, cut corners, complain, and sow destruction into our own lives? Are we being His cabinet keeper? Are we serving at His pleasure?

God will surround us with people who are like-minded. We will reap what we are sowing. What we model for others is what we will see played out in our congregations. We have to be a cabinet keeper before we will have cabinet keepers in our own lives. This is one way we can stay off the island because it forces us to sow into others' lives and trust people in return.

In 1 Samuel, we hear about a man named Abishai. He was one of David's mighty warriors. Abishai was a keeper of David and stuck to him like glue. Abishai watched as David served Saul and honored him even when Saul was trying to kill him. David was a cabinet keeper to Saul, and in turn, reaped a cabinet keeper in Abishai. He loved David as if his life depended on it just like our verse at the beginning of this chapter states.

You can read about many more mighty men in David's inner circle in 2 Samuel 22 & 23. Because of his loyalty and integrity, David reaped great people surrounding him. David didn't just trust the first person that came along. He tested people and vetted them thoroughly. They had to prove they were trustworthy people. We have to do the same.

From Robin:

I never miss church; I am always there. This one particular week I was having a hard time and was very sad. I decided on a Wednesday morning to go visit my mother who lives hours away. I didn't return until church was ending. I had gotten several texts from my friend at church, Amy, wanting to know where I was. Instead of going to church or answering her texts I went home to be by myself. I went to my house, laid across the bed and just had a good cry. We live very near the church so Amy came over and wanted to know what happened and why I wasn't at church. I know she could sense something wasn't right with me. She laid across the bed with me and I was able to cry and let my guard down a little bit. It was nice to allow Amy to minister to me. She rubbed my back and reminded me how God had me and Jerry, would keep us, and help us through this time. The roles were completely reversed, and I was able to just be a human in front of Amy. We have been dear friends ever since. Amy is one of my most trusted cabinet keepers. I also have a friend named Anna who has been there for me for over 25 years. I can share anything with her and know she will always protect me. One night I called her, and the Holy Spirit started to minister to us both. He allowed a lot of healing to happen that night and before we knew it we had been on the phone for hours. She is one of my most trusted friends and a true gift from God.

Go Where You're Celebrated

Sheila's husband Jack says quite often, "Go where you're celebrated!" In other words, hang out with the people who like you. Don't go into the areas where you are setting yourself up to be talked about, manipulated, or betrayed. God gave us discernment for our protection. Certain people mean us harm. Most of the time we know who these people are and can steer clear of them. Hang out with the people who celebrate you, not tolerate you.

From Sheila:

Several years ago, I went through a season of burnout. I was closer to being completely done with ministry than anyone knows and closer than I want to admit. I really thought I was going to lose my mind if I didn't get out of the situation I was in. People had gotten the best of me, and I was done. I remember thinking one day, "I don't have a single person I can talk to about where I am, except maybe Robin." But immediately I went through the litany of reasons why I would never call and dump all my junk on her.

God is so good because the very next day Robin called me and said, "God spoke to me in church yesterday and told me you were absolutely miserable. What can I help you with, Sis?" Well, as you can imagine the dam broke, and I could

hardly speak I was crying so hard. She ended up driving an hour and a half to meet me between our houses and let me dump the truckload of baggage I had been carrying.

She was the first person I had been completely transparent with, and it felt so good to be open and honest with someone. I knew I could trust her, but for some reason, I was keeping quiet and allowing myself to be carted off to the island. She brought me back to reality that day. She reminded me of things in God's Word I was unable to recall because my mind was so messed up. She spoke to me very pointedly and got me started on the process of getting back on the right track. I will forever be grateful to her for not letting me quit. Robin is one of my most trusted cabinet keepers.

Instead of escaping our lives through food and movies, we can create a life we don't want to escape from. We can fill our lives with people who celebrate life with us, who appreciate who we are and what we have to give.

Inventory Time

The first step is ours though. Let's take a personal inventory and answer these questions.

• Am I serving at the pleasure of the Lord?

• If I wasn't the pastor's wife would I do things the same way?

• Am I modeling the behaviors I want to see in my church family?

• Am I purposefully vetting people who could be in my cabinet?

• Am I being a keeper of others?

• Am I staying true to who God called me to be?

Be honest with yourself as you answer these questions. We can only live off the island to the extent we are honest with ourselves.

Robin has a saying that goes, "The longer you justify your behavior, the longer you give it license to stay." If you want cabinet keepers in your own life, take the time to be one first in another's life.

ANSWER & APPLY

1. Did I answer the above questions?

2. Was I completely honest with my answers?

3. What is one action I can take this week to begin to build a cabinet of trusted friends? Remember…we reap what we sow, so be a Cabinet Keeper to another first.

TAKEAWAY

God never intended for us to try and handle things on our own. He is and has always been a breath away. I would say most of the time He's waiting on us to let go of our pride and frustration. He's navigating us through our pain so we will enter into our secret place, our personal war room.

The problem is we often feel the need to be strong for everyone else. We listen to their challenges and try to help them through it. When we find ourselves in a similar situation, we shut down or refuse to share. Is being hurt and betrayed a possibility? Yes it is. But, more than likely, God will show you the people you can trust. To be the healthy women of God He called us to be, we must allow others into our world. Find your cabinet keepers and give yourself permission to be real. Life was meant to be shared.

"In our stillness, in the midst of our unanswered questions, if we'll focus on developing relationships, God will bring people across our paths who hold our answers. And as we are building those connections, God is using us to answer others' questions. Our vital interconnection is undeniably necessary, even if we refuse to engage."

In the Stillness by Deborah Stricklin

Chapter Thirteen
Making Friends With Pain

"For God is not unjust. He will not forget how hard you
have worked for Him and how you have shown your love
to Him by caring for other believers as you still do."

Hebrews 6:10

I think we can all agree what we have learned in this book is that there will be some degree of pain throughout our leadership tenure. This is life, and life in the spotlight tends to hold a certainty of difficult times. Making friends with this pain will determine our degree of success or failure.

If we look at pain as an enemy to our soul then we will avoid it, block it, hate it, and lose sight of what God wants to work in us through the pain. Realizing God is not unjust and that HE remembers the hard work you do, grants us peace in the midst of our pain.

When we allow hurtful comments, betrayals, and unrealistic expectations to settle on us, then the enemy wins and we sail for our island. When we recognize pain is coming and we embrace it, learn from it, and allow it to help us grow, then we are becoming the leader God has called us to be!

Brian Houston of Hillsong Church has a quote that we love, "If Jesus has given us the Spirit of an overcomer then we have no real excuse to live our lives offended or as the victim of someone else's opposition or pain." Is that good or what? We have no excuse. People will be people. But YOU are a leader living out an extraordinary call on behalf of the Creator of the Universe. Now is your time to shine and live as the salt and light on the mainland, not in obscurity and isolation on some lonely island. This is your time in the spotlight. Embrace this light, grasp this assignment to lead, and live your life out loud for the audience of One.

FROM SHEILA:

In 2015, I went through a season of burnout. I have eluded to it throughout the book, but I want to share an excerpt from a blog post I wrote during this time. It captures how I let the pain of leadership pile up on me and how I became undone. I took my eyes off the prize and instead was focused on myself. This led to complete and total burnout. I hope this blog will give you an understanding of what happens when we do not make friends with our pain.

"I just came off a 3-week sabbatical where I removed myself from everything and everybody. It's amazing how much you can accomplish with no phone, no social media, no work, and no appointments. I realized I needed this adult "time out" to process some things that had happened over the last 8 years since we planted a church. Before we planted we talked to some dear friends of ours, (Beth and Aaron who are also some of our most trusted cabinet keepers), who had started a church about a year before us. We asked them to tell us what we didn't know. I will never forget my friend saying these words to me, "You'll make more enemies than you ever dreamed."

Fast forward 8 years later, and I was in a place of believing we had more people who hated us than loved us. I could have never dreamed of the amount of people we would tick off, sometimes just by our very presence. I could detail for you story after story of the lies, the betrayal, the rejection, and the anger from people we considered friends,

that said they would stick by us through thick or thin.
I became very disillusioned through this process to
the point of fantasizing about moving to a foreign
country, going off the grid, or moving to a remote cabin
in Montana, growing all our own food and learning
how to sew. You know it's bad if I was thinking
about domesticating.

So here I was, 8 years later. I felt finished. Depleted. Done. I
had tried everything I knew to do to fix myself and
nothing was working. I had watched my husband over
the last year head up the construction of our new church
building. It was so stressful on him! I literally laid
awake at night sometimes, worrying if he was going to die.
Being a part of this process did not help me and where I was
headed. We were both a mess and needed a break, so
I had the idea of a sabbatical. The church completely
understood and even recognized we looked tired.

Off we went into the land of burner phones and empty cal-
endars. Even now as I write this I'm sitting in a cabin
in the woods (not in Montana) soaking in the sun,
squeezing every last minute out of my time. And I'm
seeing more clearly as to the cause of my distress. Here
are the top 3 reasons my life led to burnout.

1. Stuffing.

As a pastor's wife, it's kind of an unwritten rule that we don't get in the middle of church conflicts unless they involve us. It's hard, though, to sit by quietly and be the good little wife when someone is railing on the hubs unjustly. I believed I needed to be quiet, and in most cases, I still should! But one thing I failed to do is deal with those unresolved feelings of anger, resentment, and betrayal I felt from these people. Instead of pulling out how I felt and dealing with the pain before the Lord, I allowed these people into my mind and heart. The pain festered into an unresolved wound. The way I have always handled conflict is, we talk and get it worked out, and then we love each other again. But when the conflict isn't with me, but rather with the church that I love, or my husband, who I love, even more, I'm unable to do that.

I have to find another way to deal with this pain, and it is through releasing it to God. The people who leave us are not our enemies (some people leave correctly and are still wonderful friends), even though they may act like it. They may treat us and think of us as an enemy, but they only become my enemy if I decide they are. The real enemy is the power behind their actions; a very real devil who wants to upset us and keep us in turmoil and distracted from the ministry He has called us to complete. Years of stuffing this type of pain led to many, many layers of hurt that finally toppled into an ugly mess. When someone you love walks out of your life, do not stuff those feelings down any longer. Pull them out, grieve the loss, forgive them, and move on to the people who God has put before you.

2. Guarding.

In my mind, I knew I needed to love people. But loving people, letting them into my life, getting into their lives, and working through the muck and mire together was what led to the pain I was feeling. Several of these people left me, and I felt myself backing away, guarding my heart, guarding my actions, guarding my words, and feeling suspicious of every move. It led to me being guarded with God. If God called us to start this church, then why was so much pain involved in the process? The process was what I could not back away from. I had to stay engaged and love people regardless of how they loved me back. Men and women have been brought into our lives for a season. If someone is standing in front of me who needs my help, I need to give it. I cannot expect their loyalty, their friendship, their commitment or anything else in return. I need to give of myself and allow God to do the rest. If God has brought them before me for this time then He trusts me to help them. He believes there is something I can give that will better their life. So instead of backing away to avoid pain and thinking only of myself, I have to dive into the process and embrace the friendship and everything that comes along

with it. Guarding myself leads to isolation, and that is all the devil needs to strike, an isolated heart and mind.

3. People-pleasing.

Don't pass by this paragraph thinking this does not pertain to you. It does. Or it will. I have a tendency to remember the negative. I can have 999 people I just spoke to tell me what a great job I did; 1 says something negative, and I go home and obsess about the negative. It's the same with the church. Remembering these hurtful words led to me altering my behavior, my clothes, and my actions to please different people who had said different things. I never saw that as people pleasing; I started out thinking I was helping the church and being a good pastor's wife. But in the process somehow, I lost myself. I ended up being this person I didn't like very much because I was just bland, gray, non-adventurous, saintly Sheila. I allowed others to set the rules, and I bent over backward to follow everyone else's rules for me. I'm recognizing this and I'm trying to work out of it. I'm still discovering the areas in which I have allowed others' expectations to rule.

These three areas are what I have pinpointed as what led to my demise. I don't like sounding so negative like being a pastor's wife is all this and nothing else. The positive moments equal no other, like when

someone has been through a harrowing circumstance and they call for help because they trust you more than anyone else. That is a privilege that still to this day brings tears to my eyes. That moment never grows old. There are people who left a good, secure, church (the right way) and came with us to the unknown to plant a new church, and they are still with us today. These people are our lifeline. They hold up our arms. They pray for us; they are trusted, friends. I could write a novel on the moments over the last 8 years that I will treasure forever.

What I know for sure is there will always be people I have to keep my mouth quiet about…there will always be people the Holy Spirit warns me to guard myself around…and there will be times I need to get over myself and please other people. This is life, and it's not all bad. Recognizing these things in my life, and their out of control state, has helped me pinpoint my turnaround spot.

While on this 3-week adventure I read 2 books, *Leadership Pain* by Sam Chand and *When Words Hurt* by Warren Bullock. I would recommend both books. Sam Chand says, "You'll grow only to the threshold of your pain." Those are incredible words of wisdom.

We cannot say enough about Sam Chand's book, *Leadership Pain*. When we think of growing only to the threshold of our pain, then pain becomes a different thing all together.

WASTED DAYS AND WASTED NIGHTS

We all know in God's Kingdom nothing is wasted. That holds true with pain, too. Time after time there have been examples all through God's Word of people who went through very difficult, painful times that led to incredible victories. We can choose to waste day after day and night after night wallowing in pain and feeling sorry for ourselves, or we can choose to live in victory. We are not victims in the hands of other people. We are overcomers made victorious by the hand of God!

FROM ROBIN:

In 2015 my aunt died that I was very close to. Everything she represented was huge to me. My uncle, her husband, died just weeks later. Their daughter, my cousin, died 6 weeks after that. My remaining cousin in this family was devastated as you can imagine. Our whole family is still reeling from the weight of these losses. During all of this, a precious family in our church lost their son from a drug overdose. This young man was a new member of our church and was doing well, so this was devastating to our church and weighed on Jerry and me tremendously. Just a few weeks after that, my best friend from our church left the church, and then a member of our staff dealt with a moral failure. While this was all happening another member of our staff was dealing with serious marital issues. I would lay awake at night and cry. It was all I could do, I felt so heavy and sad. During this time, I felt God's presence, but directionally I felt His silence. When my mind became clear enough to hear Him, He showed me two important truths that I want to share with you.

ONE.

When we are in the middle of a painful storm, transition is likely to soon follow. This transition can happen emotionally, physically, mentally, or positionally as God is preparing to shift you. If you are in pain, that is a sign something is going on that is bigger than you. Just like when a storm is on its way in nature, there are always signs. Black clouds roll in, and the wind starts blowing. It's the same in the physical. Signs start showing up and we can know it's only temporal. This pain is a storm that will pass. We have to embrace the pain because it tells us God is up to something. The enemy always whispers his lies that we're not good enough, or we're not doing a good job during this time. We have to know the Father's voice, or we will be drawn away to the island by those lies.

Two.

This is not just a lesson we're learning, but this pain is for other people watching you, too. People may not recognize it verbally, but they are watching to see if you are going to remain faithful. We are teaching people how to process pain while we're processing pain. We're learning in real time; learning as we're teaching. Going through a storm does not produce your character; it reveals your character to yourself and others. Sometimes a storm uncovers ugliness inside us, and it provides the opportunity to purge the unwanted actions, the ugly imaginings or mindsets from our lives. I've learned to understand that sometimes it doesn't make sense, I feel desperate, and I need direction. As a result of recognizing these red flags and feelings, I am reminded He is still in control. He is still moving whether or not we are aware of it.

We have to be intentional in these moments. If we are not purposeful about taking the time to listen to God, then most likely we will miss what He wants us to understand about our current situation.

ONE OF THE TOP 10

One of the ways we avoid burnout and being bogged down by pain is by implementing a weekly Sabbath. Do you think God needed to rest on the 7th day? No. He's God. We are not. He wanted us to learn by His example. If He also included this command in the top 10 directives for our lives, then it must be PREEETY important.

Sabbath rest is no laughing matter. It is also something we cannot blow off as unimportant. We can't wait until our health goes bad, or we suffer burnout, or we become toxic before we allow ourselves to rest. We must rest even when we don't feel like we need it. You may be on top of the world with everything going great in your life, but that doesn't mean it is not necessary for you to take a day off. Sabbath rest is not just needed when everything falls apart, but it is also for when we are at the top of our game.

Mark 2:27 says, "Then Jesus said to them. The Sabbath was made to meet the needs of the people, and not people to meet the requirements of the Sabbath." There isn't some legalistic way in which we have to spend the Sabbath. If your resting looks like playing golf, then do it. If your resting looks like pitching a tent and camping for the night, then do it. If your resting looks like shopping, or painting, or laying in bed with a good book, then do it. Just allow yourself to rest with no guilt. And, be assured through this rest you are pleasing to God, showing Him your love for His commands. He will help you rest from any pain in your life and you will be more fit to make it through each day and every situation.

Rick Warren once said, "Divert daily, withdraw weekly, and abandon annually." That means turn off your phone every day and get away from the stresses of work and the church. Withdraw to your resting place every week. But then abandon everything for an extended period of time every year. Now that's a program we can follow, right Ladies?

Taking time to rest helps us in the moments of pain that we will need to grow through. Here is another quote by Sam Chand from his book, Leadership Pain, "Facing pain may require more courage than we've ever had in our lives. At many different points, maybe even today, I can guarantee that you will reach the threshold of your pain and think, I've had it that's all I can take! Get me out of here! But it's not over. You've simply turned the next page in your life's story of excellent leadership. You're at this moment because you have successfully navigated many types of hurt, loss, grief, betrayal, and complexity. You've raised your pain threshold many times in the past. It's time to raise it again."

And this Ladies is how we live off the island. We remain steadfast regardless of circumstances because we have an Audience of One who has called us to this task. There is a greater cause at stake than you and I can fully realize this side of heaven. The mission is always greater than our personal pain. We must not be swayed, we must not back down, and we must not sail away. A hurting world needs our gifts, our words, our compassion, our kindness, our very lives, and we must be willing to give it...even through the pain.

ANSWER & APPLY

1. What purpose does my pain have?

2. Does that purpose lead me toward God or away from God?

3. Does that purpose lead me toward others or away from others?

4. What is one thing I have learned about pain?

TAKEAWAY

The amount of pain we are willing to endure has a lot to do with the effectiveness of our leadership. If we will weather pain well by staying on task, it makes us better leaders. God works all things for our good, including all the storms, too! Knowledge is a keystroke away from Google, but wisdom only comes from honesty, experience, time, requesting it, and weathering pain.

IN CLOSING...

We must close with this scripture because it sums up what we have been living and saying throughout this entire book. Let's make this our mantra from this day forward!

"We live in such a way that no one will stumble because of us, and no one will find fault with our ministry. In everything we do, we show that we are true ministers of God. We patiently endure troubles and hardships and calamities of every kind. We have been beaten, been put in prison, faced angry mobs, worked to exhaustion, endured sleepless nights, and gone without food. We prove ourselves by our purity, our understanding, our patience, our kindness, by the Holy Spirit within us, and by our sincere love. We faithfully preach the truth. God's power is working in us. We use the weapons of righteousness in the right hand for attack and the left hand for defense. We serve God whether people honor us or despise us, whether they slander us or praise us. We are honest, but they call us impostors. We are ignored, even though we are well known. We live close to death, but we are still alive. We have been beaten, but we have not been killed. Our hearts ache, but we always have joy. We are poor, but we give spiritual riches to others. We own nothing, but yet we have everything."

2 CORINTHIANS 6:3-10

ABOUT YOUR AUTHORS

A Little About Robin...

I've been married 33 years to Jerry, my true and only soul mate. Together we have three children and three beautiful grandchildren. Like my friend Sheila, we also have a dog. Her name is Buttons, and to be honest I probably should have told you we have four children instead of three. She thinks she is human. Jerry and I met when I was sixteen, and we were dating each other's best friends! As God would have it we realized we liked each other more than we liked our current boy/girlfriend, so we switched, and we've been together ever since.

To give you a little information about myself, wait- let me back up a bit and tell you I've been in ministry my whole life. My grandfather, father, husband, and various relatives were and are denominational leaders, evangelists, and pastors. All I've known is ministry, the joy and sometimes hurt of helping people.

As a child growing up with my dad as the state overseer for our denomination, I visited hundreds of churches. My father would often speak at three or four a week. We would travel many miles doing ministry every weekend. Because of his schedule, we didn't take off much or go on many vacations. When we did take time off, it usually was a couple of days in Florida hanging out with relatives. We lived and breathed church work. I would be safe to say ministry consumed our lives. I saw many "not so great" moments in people's lives, and yet I still felt this yearning to dive in and give God everything I had.

When I was sixteen years old my dad was appointed the General Director of Publications in our denomination so our family moved to Cleveland, Tennessee. Because he didn't travel as much on weekends, I finally got to attend the same church for four years. This is where I met Jerry who so many now fondly call PJ (Pastor Jerry).

Jerry and I dated on and off all through high school and college and eventually married and immediately went into full-time ministry. You would think because of all the experience I had, going into full-time ministry as an adult would be a piece of cake. Wrong! It was like starting fresh and learning a whole new world. This world was filled with heartbreaks and challenges I had only witnessed from a child's perspective.

The first ten or so years of our ministry were spent in various associate positions. Somewhere around our fifteenth year, we became full-time music pastors. We were on national and state music boards, teen talent committees, and many regional groups. The Lord birthed in my husband a "Passion Play" while we served as Worship and Arts Pastors in Rome, Georgia. This production eventually had over five hundred cast and crew, and eighteen thousand people attended. Hundreds were saved, and it was probably the pinnacle of our musical years.

In 2005, the Lord spoke to us again and led Jerry to get his Masters of Divinity degree to become a lead pastor.

This is where everything changed.

Once we stepped into this new season, the game was on. The enemy had a plan to discourage us and get us to throw in the towel. No one, and I mean no one, prepares you for the weight you carry, the disappointment you face, and the bombardment the enemy sends your way. But, God had and always has a plan.

In 2012, the Lord spoke to me and reminded me I had always had a heart for pastors and leaders. Not until I became a lead pastor's wife did I realize what an opportunity God was giving me. That opportunity was a ministry forming called Destiny Pastors.

Our first meeting was with Jack and Sheila Harper. What a validating experience that was! You see, I felt like pastors needed a place, a forum, to open up about their challenges and their victories. In one weekend of bearing our souls with each other, He created this new and exciting ministry.

Four months later, six couples came together and shared on a level not previously realized. The four of us walked away from that weekend realizing this type of forum is desperately needed among pastors. But I had one large challenge. What about all the other pastors and their wives? What about the thousands of women out there who felt like they were drowning and wanted to give up and never do ministry again?

This is the reason for writing this book; it's for you, the pastor's wife. By the time you finish reading, our prayer is you'll press in and allow the Lord to light your fire to a level it's never been lit before.

If you have this book in your possession then God has something in store for you. So, here is our story. We can't wait to hear yours!

A Little About Sheila...

My story could not be more opposite than Robin's. I wish I could tell you I was raised in the church and made good decisions. You will soon learn that has not been the case in my life.

To tell you a little about my current day life, I have been married to Jack for 28 years, and we have two wonderful boys named Jarod and Jakob. We also have a really cool, but annoying dog named Judah. My boys are both grown, but seem to be unphased by the fact I want grandkids and that they need to get married and have me some. They are wonderful boys and have a great sense of adventure they get from me. Jack is the strong, even-tempered, rock of the family. He is the glue that holds all of us together. If he gets upset then we know something is terribly wrong and the world has fallen off its axis! My boys wakeboard, snowboard, skydive, rock climb, travel, do missions work overseas and squeeze every ounce of life they can out of each day. I'm very proud of my boys and my husband, and I'm thrilled I get to be their mom and wife.

In my professional life, Jack and I started a business back in 1996. We were working insurance claims for several different insurance companies. We had a team of adjusters who worked for our company, and we loved life. I drove a Mercedes, carried $300 purses, had a pool in my backyard behind my big ole house. We went on killer vacations, sent our kids to private school, and just felt like we had arrived. We were living the dream and having great success.

During this time, the church we attended asked Jack to teach a Bible study class in the year 2000. The thought was so foreign to us, but we said yes because we were young Christians and wanted to do everything we could for God. The first week he taught we had 52 people in the class. The 2nd week…26. We ran half the class away!

He finally fell into a groove, and we started realizing he had a real knack for writing and speaking. He was just learning the Bible, and I truly believe because we got started so late in life that God made Jack's mind like a sponge. He could retain so much of God's Word. It was a beautiful thing to see my husband change like he did.

Again, we had great success with this Bible study class. We started growing, and within a couple of years grew this class to 200 people. We raised up a leader from those 200; the church split the class and formed a new one. That happened repeatedly during the 7 years we taught that class, until more than half of all the classes at the church were splits from our class. We loved seeing people grow in the Lord, and we truly loved teaching them and pouring into their lives.

From 2003 until 2007 Jack felt as though God was calling him to more. We both felt it, but we weren't sure what it was until God made it clear. He wanted us to plant a church.

We talked to our pastor, and he confirmed that he believed the same thing should happen. He pointed Jack in the direction of how to get his education and credentials. Jack followed those instructions and waited on our pastor's leading as to when he felt as though we were ready to launch out.

In November of 2007, we got rid of the adjusting business and put everything we had into planting Crossroads Church.

God did a number on me, as my heart was changing and no longer wanted the material possessions I thought were so important before. It was a good thing because Jack started his new salary, and it was exactly one-quarter of what he made the year before. This was going to be a new, radical chapter in our lives, and we were ready to embrace it.

Everything we touched before had turned to gold, and we were expecting nothing less from this church and its success.

In the meantime, I also had started a ministry called SaveOne, that I truly thought would be nothing more than a Bible study I taught at my church. It was birthed from the pain and regret of my own abortion in 1985.

SaveOne is an abortion recovery ministry. We help men, women, and families recover after abortion. We believe at SaveOne it is how we will end abortion in our country and around our world. Again, we've had incredible success with this ministry and as of this writing, we have nearly 200 chapters of SaveOne in eighteen different countries.

So far, I have written six books.

I have traveled the world training new leaders to teach the SaveOne Bible studies, and speaking to pastors about the effects of abortion on men, women, and families. I have partnered with many churches educating them on how we can fight the abortion issue through love and acceptance and no longer with judgment, controversy, or politics. You can check out all we are doing at www. saveone.org

But back to the church. We are many years into this church plant, and I can easily say it is by far the most difficult job we have ever had. Mix the struggles of the church with feeling like I'm all alone and can't truly talk to anyone, and it's a dangerous combination. This is one of the reasons why I felt this book was necessary. I know there are other pastors' wives who have found themselves in my shoes.

We have to believe in each other along the way and give a high five or spirit fingers to each other to encourage and say, "DON'T GIVE UP! God has you in His righteous right hand, and He is intimately interested in every detail of your life!"

So that is a little about me. Robin and I would love to hear from you. Our email address is on the back cover. So, when you're through reading this book will you write and tell us your story? We want to hear from you!

AND THE CREDIT GOES TO ...

AND ROBIN WANTS
TO GIVE CREDIT TO...

My Lord and Savior Jesus Christ, who always rights my path
and rescues me when I'm headed for the island!

My husband, Jerry, for believing in me
and loving me through the process.

My parents, Oliver and Ruth McCane for telling me
for 20 years they knew I was destined to write a book
and for praying for me all these years.

My children, Matthew, Cara, Steven, Erin, Brian,
and Lauren for encouraging me to fulfill my dream.

My best friends, Anna Burt and Amy Pilgrim
for allowing me to vent and protect me at all costs.
You have been my cabinet keepers.

Every church we have served, you taught us more than words can express.

And lastly my friend Sheila Harper for taking a year of her life and
partnering with me to walk out our dream to help women in ministry.

Thanks to my friends and fellow pastor's wives
Anna Burt, Patti Wright, and Amy Pilgrim, for editing this book.
I love all of you with my whole heart!

And Sheila wants
to give credit to...

My Lord and Savior Jesus Christ, for without
Him none of this would be possible.

My wonderful husband, Jack, who has listened
to me whine when I didn't feel like I could write, but
always pointed me back in the direction of my dreams.

My boys, Jarod and Jakob, who inspire me to be more a
dventurous, dare me to do crazy things, spur me on to
believe bigger, keep me on my knees with their antics,
and indulge my stories about life.

My IFQ's who remain steadfast in my life and are just a
text away from setting off a powerful prayer chain for each other.

Thanks to my friends and fellow pastor's wives
Debbie Thompson, Deborah Stricklin, and Vanessa McGee,
for editing this book. Your wisdom was invaluable!

And lastly, my friend, Robin Gilliam, who has encouraged me,
been my trusted cabinet keeper, indulged my tearful hurts,
and reminded me who I am in Christ and that what
we've been called to is bigger than all of us!

I love all of you with my whole heart!